# Discovering the FOUR SEASONS

*Why do birds fly in V patterns?

*How can a sunset help
you predict the weather?

# Discovering
## the
# FOUR
# SEASONS

◆ ◆ ◆

**Jeffery Scott Wallace**

**Lion Publishing**
Oxford ◆ Batavia◆ Sydney

*What do you need to make your own paper?

Text copyright © 1994 by Jeffery Scott Wallace
Illustrations © 1994 by Scott Holladay

Design by Terry Julien

Published by
**Lion Publishing**
20 Lincoln Avenue, Elgin, IL 60120, USA
ISBN 0 7459 2617 7
**Lion Publishing plc**
Sandy Lane West, Oxford, England
ISBN 0 7459 2617 7
**Albatross Books Pty**
PO Box 320, Sutherland, NSW 2232, Australia
ISBN 0 7324 0677 3

First edition 1994

**Library of Congress Cataloging-in-Publication Data**
Wallace, Jeffery Scott, 1960-
    Discovering the Four Seasons / by Jeffery Scott Wallace.
       p.   cm. — (Creation up close)
    Summary: Presents facts, historical trivia, folklore, and activities related
to the four seasons and discusses how to care for God's gift of nature.
    ISBN 0-7459-2617-7 : $7.99
    1. Seasons—Juvenile literature. [1. Seasons.   2. Christian life.]   I. Title.   II. Series.
QB637. 4. W33  1993                         92-43796
508—dc20                                    CIP
                                            AC

A catalogue record for this book is available from the British Library

Printed and bound in USA

# CONTENTS

*Do moose really migrate?

• • • • • • • • • • • • • • • • • • • • • • • • • • • • • • • • • • • • •

To Nathaniel and Gracie,
who bring joy to all the seasons of my life
◆ ◆ ◆

*What causes bears
to hibernate?

# Introduction

This is a book about discovering. It will give you a hands-on, up-close look at the amazing world in which you live. Take it along as you explore. It will come in handy when you wonder why ants live together in colonies, why birds fly south for the winter, or why green leaves turn yellow, orange, and red in autumn. It will also tell you where pumpkin lanterns come from and how to know when rainy weather is on the way.

This is also a book about seasons—about the wind in spring, the sun in summer, the trees in autumn, and the snow in winter. You'll learn about April Fools' Day, Easter, Halloween, and Christmas.

But this is more than just a book about the seasons. It's really about life and enjoying life. When God made the earth, he created a home for an awesome variety of living things. And all these creatures depend on each other for survival. As you explore the four seasons, you will meet some fascinating creatures that depend on you. And you'll discover ways in which you depend on other creatures—ways that may surprise you. You'll also find out how you can help care for the earth and its creatures.

And you will discover how much fun it can be to view creation up close.

# Chapter 1

# Springing into Life

## Reason for the Season

What causes a season to be spring, summer, autumn, or winter? Every season depends on two things: the earth's movement around the sun and the tilt of the earth as it moves.

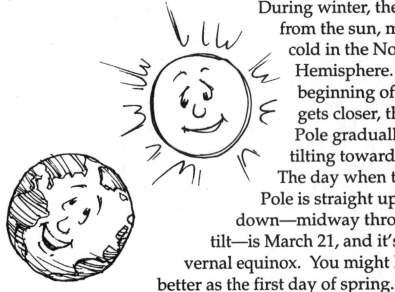

During winter, the North Pole is tilted away from the sun, making it cold in the Northern Hemisphere. But as the beginning of spring gets closer, the North Pole gradually starts tilting toward the sun. The day when the North Pole is straight up and down—midway through its tilt—is March 21, and it's called the vernal equinox. You might know it better as the first day of spring.

Even though spring doesn't officially start until March 21, sometimes you can discover hints of spring during the last weeks of winter.

Look in the flower bed around your home. Are there light green tips poking through the ground? These could well be tulips and daffodils, letting you know that spring isn't far off. Do you have willow and birch trees nearby? Are buds appearing on their branches? These trees are among the first every year to sprout leaves. On a warm day, sit down outside and listen carefully. Can you hear the croaking of a few frogs? How about the buzzing of some early insects? Hear the chirping of any young birds? These are signs that spring is close. The world is waking up!

## Warm-Up Time!

People used to think that heat from the sun warmed the air and that warm air was what made the temperature go up every spring. But that's not really true.

Sunlight doesn't warm the air as it passes through it, but sunlight does warm the earth's surface. The ground absorbs the heat from the sun, then radiates that heat up into the air. Clouds and other air-pressure systems trap that warm air between the earth and the sky so that it doesn't disappear into space.

The more daylight hours the sun has to warm up the earth's surface, the warmer the air gets. So as the days grow longer in spring, the air grows warmer, and the temperature goes up.

## Pollination:
## Flowers and Insects Working Together

Trees and plants were created to make flowers all by themselves. But the flowers of some trees and plants go on to become fruits and vegetables later in the year. That only happens when a flower makes seeds—something for the fruit or vegetable to grow around. And the only way flowers can make seeds is through a process called pollination.

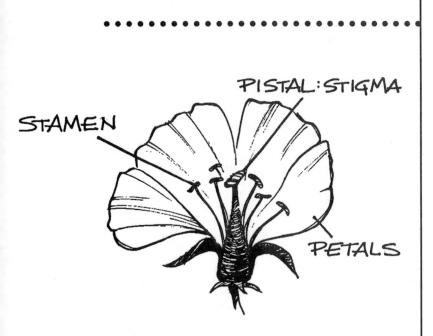

STAMEN

PISTAL:STIGMA

PETALS

Inside the flowers of trees and plants are male parts and female parts. Unless those parts can be fertilized, or "pollinated," there will be no seed. No seeds, no fruits or vegetables.

Unlike animals, trees and plants can't roam around the forest or the garden looking for a mate. Instead, a seed is produced when pollen is carried from the male part of one flower to the female part of another flower of the same type. Pollen—a tiny, grain-like powder that is usually yellow—is created in the male part, called the stamen. One way or another, that pollen must find its way to the female part, called the pistil. The process of getting the pollen from the stamen to the pistil is what pollination is all about.

Some flowers don't need any help getting pollen from the stamen to the pistil. They're called self-pollinating flowers—they have both a stamen and a pistil.

In these kinds of flowers, the pollen simply drops from the stamen to the top part of the pistil—called the stigma. The stigma absorbs the pollen, carries it down the trunk of the pistil, and begins the process of making seeds. Wheat, peas, oats, and barley are some of the plants that can pollinate themselves.

Some flowers, like lilies and hibiscuses, have both a stamen and a pistil, but they don't self-pollinate. Why? Because the stamen is shorter than the pistil. When the stamen drops pollen, it just falls to the bottom of the flower. Apparently, these flowers would rather let someone—or something—do their work for them!

## With a Little Help from Some Friends

Most flowers depend on helpers to carry pollen from a male flower to a female flower. They're called cross-pollinating flowers.

Some cross-pollinating flowers rely on the wind to spread their pollen around, so these flowers usually create millions of pollen grains. It's as if they realize that a lot of the pollen carried by the wind will never make it to the right flowers. The more pollen they make, the better their chances!

In the spring, it is easy to spot the pollen from these flowers. Pollen grains might cover a car sitting beneath an oak tree. Or dusty yellow grains could be floating in a puddle of water near ragweed. Brush your hand across the top of some wild grasses, and watch clumps of pollen particles fly. These flowers leave pollen everywhere!

## ALLERGIC TO SPRING

Because of pollen, some people can be miserable during spring. Those with pollen allergies (commonly known as "hay fever") experience a runny nose, sneezing, and itchy eyes. Pollen is the most common cause of allergic reactions. Yet, pollen is the hardest kind of allergy-causing substance to avoid. Its particles can be so small that you can't even see them as they float in the air. You can breathe them in without even knowing it.

If you are allergic to pollen, don't give up hope. Just wait for the next rain. A good spring downpour naturally cleans the air of these sometimes pesky particles.

## Bugs, Bees, and Birds

Insects are cross-pollinating flowers' best friends. A few kinds of wasps, beetles, flies, butterflies, moths, and bees all play a part in pollination.

How do they do it?

Insects are attracted to flowers because they like to eat pollen and nectar, the sweet liquid created inside a flower. Pollen is usually an insect's main course; it's rich in proteins as well as vitamins and minerals. Nectar is the insect's dessert.

When an insect crawls into a flower for a snack, it almost always brushes against parts of the flower. As it moves against the stamen of a male flower, pollen sticks to the hairs on its body. Then, when that insect goes to a female flower (of the same kind) for another snack, its hairs brush against the pistil—leaving pollen on the stigma. Every time this happens, the flower can begin to form seeds.

Birds also are friends of cross-pollinating flowers. Some birds like to sip the nectar from flowers. As they do, pollen clings to their heads and feathers. These birds then carry the pollen from one flower to another the same way insects do.

## From Nectar to Honey

When a bee visits a flower and sips nectar from it, the bee doesn't just swallow all the sugary nectar and get fat. The bee stores the nectar in a

*Why are bees considered among flowers' best friends?*

Bees have a habit of feeding at the same kind of flower. So, the pollen that sticks to their stiff body hairs is more likely to be brushed off onto another flower of that same kind of plant.

Most flowers pollinated by insects and birds are heavily scented and brightly colored. Most flowers pollinated by the wind have neither a fragrant scent nor bright petals.

Different insects and birds are attracted by different odors and colors, and so, tend to visit specific kinds of flowers. This, in turn, increases the chances of cross-pollination from one flower to another flower of the same kind.

pouch inside its body. When this pouch—called a "honey stomach"—is full, the bee returns to its hive.

But a funny thing happens on the way to the hive. While the bee buzzes homeward, a complex process called "inversion" is happening in its honey stomach. Inversion breaks down the nectar into two kinds of sugar—fructose and glucose. By the time the bee arrives at its hive, the process is complete.

Once home, the bee empties the contents of its honey stomach into tiny, waxy, six-sided containers. The group of containers within the beehive is called a "comb."

Stored away in the comb, the watery portion of the nectar evaporates, leaving a thick, sticky liquid: honey.

When thousands of bees work together, they soon store up enough honey to feed every bee in the hive—and lots of people, too! That's why good beekeepers always remember to leave some honey for the bees to eat when they collect honey from the combs.

# Chapter 2
# Celebrating Spring

### Tulip Time!

One of the most popular heralds of spring is the tulip. Tulips grow from bulbs that must be planted in the late summer or autumn. From these bulbs, several leaves and a stem develop. They usually pop through the ground in late winter, trumpeting the fact that spring will soon be coming.

The tulip plant grows quickly. As it grows, a green oval will form at the end of the stem. Within a few weeks, the oval bursts open and reveals one of the prettiest of all flowers.

## A TULIP BY ANY OTHER NAME

The name "tulip" comes from a Turkish word that means "turban." Apparently when some people first saw this flower bloom, they thought the blossoms looked like a little turban. People began calling the flower "tulip," and it has had that name ever since.

### April Showers and May Flowers

Have you ever heard the saying, "April showers bring May flowers"? Did you know this phrase has been used for hundreds of years?

This phrase originated with a little known English poet named Thomas Tusser, who lived over four hundred years ago. In a book published in 1557, Tusser wrote these words:

*Sweet April showers*
*Do spring May flowers.*

The point Tusser was making, of course, is that the rains that fall in April enrich and nourish the ground so that, coupled with the sunshine, flowers will bloom in May.

Over time, Tusser's words changed ever so slightly, and so did their meaning. These words eventually came to be understood as a proverb: "April showers bring May flowers." As a proverb, this phrase means that unpleasant experiences can still have happy endings.

## Arbor Day

Arbor Day is a day set aside in the United States for planting trees.

Arbor Day began when American newspaper publisher Julius Sterling Morton learned how trees greatly nourish the soil and help to conserve its moisture. After planting many trees on his own, he encouraged other people in his home state of Nebraska to plant trees as well. Morton's idea caught on quickly. In fact, Nebraska declared April 10, 1872, as the first Arbor Day.

To honor Morton after his death in 1902, the date of Arbor Day was changed to Morton's birthday—April 22—and declared a holiday. Other states recognized the importance of planting trees and also began celebrating Arbor Day. Now several countries throughout the world set aside a special day for planting trees.

## Plant a Tree Day

Everyone can experience the fun of planting a tree. First, ask your parents to help you choose a place to plant a tree. Then purchase one or more tree seedlings from a local nursery. (Sometimes environmental

organizations give away seedlings to encourage people to plant trees.) Once you have your seedlings, you are ready to plant.

To plant a tree, dig a hole big enough for the roots of the seedling to spread out. As you dig, put the topsoil on one side of the hole and the subsoil, the harder dirt under the topsoil, on the other. Drive a stake into the middle of the hole. You will use this stake to support the seedling.

Place the seedling into the hole, carefully spreading its roots across the bottom. Cover the roots with topsoil. (Topsoil is more fertile than subsoil and will give the seedling a healthy start for growing into a big tree.) Then, fill in the rest of the hole with subsoil. Pat down the dirt so that it is level with the ground around it.

Use an old soft cloth to tie the top part of the seedling's trunk to the stake. Don't tie it too tightly. You only want the cloth to hold the seedling upright. Later on, as the seedling grows taller and is able to stand well on its own, you will remove the cloth and the stake.

Don't forget to water your tree every now and then—especially if it hasn't rained for a few days. The seedling, with help from the sun, soil, and rain, will do the rest. Over the next few years, you can watch your seedling grow into a full grown tree!

## The Windy Season

Spring is usually the windiest of all seasons. That's why the best time to fly a kite is in March or April. Did you ever wonder why?

The sun is actually the main cause of windy days. After a long winter, the earth's surface is cooler than at any other time of the year. At the beginning of spring, the sun starts to warm up the earth's surface again. The sun's energy is absorbed by rocks, soil, and water—even by cars, houses, and buildings. These things then release and radiate heat, warming the air close to the earth's surface.

But the warm air doesn't just hover near the ground. Warm air is light; it starts to rise away from the earth's surface. As this warm air moves higher, the heavier cool air has to move out of its way. So it rolls over and pushes under the warm air. When this happens, wind is created.

How strong the wind blows depends on how different the temperature is between the warm air near the surface and the cool air above it. During the early part of spring, the air near the surface can get warm quickly, so it will rise very fast. This warm air slams into the cold air leftover from the winter, which goes rushing back down toward the earth's surface. The result is a strong and cold spring wind.

## THE SOUNDS OF THUNDER

Many people think thunder is the sound of lightning occurring. But that's not quite true. Thunder is the sound a cloud makes when lightning heats the air inside. The hot lightning causes the cloud's air to expand, and the expanding hot air crashes into the cool air that surrounds it. The sound waves that result can be heard on the earth's surface—thunder.

## Thunder and Lightning

You've been enjoying a warm, sunny spring afternoon outdoors when the wind starts to blow harder. You look up and notice dark clouds moving across the sky. Small trees with new leaves start swaying. The grass moves in waves as the wind blows past.

Suddenly, a bolt of lightning streaks across the western sky. Seconds later, you hear a distant rumble. Then another flash— and a loud crack of thunder.

When the first raindrop pelts your arm, you know it's time to go inside. A storm is coming!

## The Charge of the Lightning Brigade

Clouds, like everything else, are made of atoms. Atoms are usually electrically neutral. But sometimes, because of light or heat, these atoms become positively or negatively charged.

Positive charges are attracted to negative charges, and so these electrical charges naturally move toward each other. When the positive and negative electrical charges move through the air toward each other, they form an electric current that causes a giant electrical spark. When this giant spark occurs, lightning is the result.

Lightning can occur from a cloud to the ground or from cloud to cloud. It can also occur inside a single cloud, making it look as if fireworks are going off inside.

## How Far Away Is the Lightning?

You always see lightning before you hear the thunder. Why? Because light travels faster than sound.

Light travels 186,282 miles per second. Sound travels 1,100 feet per second. So, if you were in London and flashed a light that could be seen by a friend in New York City, the light would reach her in one-fiftieth of a second! But if you were in London and clapped your hands so that the sound could be heard by your friend in New York, it would take five hours, twenty-five minutes, and fifteen seconds for her to hear the sound.

It is easy to figure out the distance between you and a lightning strike. When you see a bolt of lightning, start counting the seconds. When you hear the thunder from that lightning strike, stop. Divide the number of seconds you counted by five. The result is the number of miles away the lightning strike was.

## LEGENDARY LIGHTNING (AND THUNDER)

When the ancient Greeks and Romans heard thunder crashing all around them, they believed the thunder to be the voice of the god Zeus, who was angrily scolding them. Later, Scandinavian people believed lightning was created when the god Thor struck his anvil with his mighty hammer. The sound of the hammering created thunder.

More recent legends have suggested that thunder is made by tiny people playing ninepins—a bowling game—in the heavens. Rumbling thunder is made when the ball rolls toward the pins. Loud, crashing thunder occurs when the ball knocks all the pins over.

## April Fools' Day

Have you ever had a joke played on you on April Fools' Day—the first day of April? Or maybe you played a joke on someone else? How did all of this foolishness get started?

The *Poor Robin's Almanac* of 1760 asked that question too. But the answer wasn't much help for the readers who wondered about what they called "All Fools' Day":

*The first of April, some do say*
*Is set apart for All Fools' Day;*
*But why the people call it so*
*Nor I, nor they themselves, do know.*

April Fools' Day actually began in France during the sixteenth century. In 1564, King Charles IX ordered that the calendar for his nation be changed. Up to that time, the people of France celebrated New Year's Day on April 1. But when the king changed the calendar, New Year's Day fell on January 1—like it does today.

Many French people became confused over the calendar change. When they celebrated April 1 as though it were New Year's Day, they became known as "April fools."

The custom of playing pranks on these April fools soon followed. And in time, people began "fooling" their friends and family members as well. This custom became so popular that it quickly spread to other countries.

## The Story of Easter

Easter is the most important holiday of spring. It is the day Christians celebrate Jesus Christ's return to life.

The Bible tells the whole story. In the books known as Gospels (gospel means "good news") Jesus' followers Matthew, Mark, Luke, and John told how Jesus spent his life on earth healing sick people, helping poor people, and teaching people how to live a good life and follow God. He performed many miracles, such as feeding 5,000 people with only one small boy's lunch, walking on water, and even bringing dead people back to life. But some of the religious leaders of the land were offended by Jesus' life and message. They felt he was stealing their authority over people, so they plotted to have Jesus killed.

## WHY "EASTER"?

No one is quite sure how the name *Easter* came into use. Some people say *eastre* is an Old English name for the goddess of spring. It is also possible that the word referred to a spring festival, or maybe even to spring itself.

Others think the word came from the early German word *eostarun*, which means "dawn of the morning." A few people believe the word *Easter* came from the Latin word *albae*, which means both "dawn of the morning" and "white."

Their scheme finally worked. Jesus was falsely accused of treason against the Roman government. On a Friday afternoon, Jesus was nailed to a cross. He died hours later and was buried in a garden tomb.

The Bible says that Jesus was the Son of God. He was perfect and sinless. When Jesus died on the cross, he took the punishment for everyone else's sin on himself. And through his death, God could forgive people who weren't perfect and sinless. That is why Christians call the Friday before Easter "Good Friday."

After his death, Jesus' followers were heartbroken and afraid. They had lost their friend and leader. They thought they might be captured and killed as well. So they hid, and remained in hiding until Sunday morning.

On Sunday, some of Jesus' followers went to visit his tomb. But when they got there, they found that the huge stone that had sealed the entrance to the tomb had been moved. Jesus' body was gone. Just as they were about to panic, an angel told them that Jesus had risen from the dead, that he was alive again.

After that first Easter morning, Jesus met with his followers and even talked and ate with them many times. He promised them that he would give new life to everyone else who believed in him, new life now and a new life in heaven after their life on earth was finished.

Christians believe Jesus' return to life, or resurrection, on Easter means that they, too, will have new life after death. Easter is a wonderful celebration of life and hope.

## When Is Easter?

Easter doesn't come on the same date every year. It's a moveable holiday. In A.D. 325, a large group of church leaders set the method for determining the date of Easter. No one said, "Let's keep this simple," though.

The leaders decided that Easter should fall on the first Sunday after the first full moon on or after March 21—the first day of spring. It could not come before March 22 or after April 25, however.

Why did the church leaders use such a complicated method for planning Easter? Why didn't they just pick a date—like the second Sunday in April?

In those days, many people lived in the country, sometimes far away from the cities and towns where churches celebrated Easter with big festivals. To help these Christians attend the festivals, they set Easter to always follow a full moon. That way, the Christians could travel late at night—by the light of the moon—to reach the Easter festivals held at the churches.

## Symbols of Spring

*The Egg*

Long before Christians began celebrating Easter, the egg was a symbol of new life. And as a symbol of new life, it naturally became one of the symbols of spring, and so was added to the celebration of Easter.

In fact, many people living long ago used to tell a legend about how the earth was an egg before it came into being. One of those legends—from India—said the earth was formed after the egg lay for a year and then split into two parts. One of the parts was silver. The other was gold. From these two parts, the legend says, the earth took shape.

*The Bunny*

Since so many plants revive and so many animals give birth in the spring, this season above all others has come to be known as the season of new life and fertility. Rabbits, because of their ability to produce so many young in so little time, have long been a symbol of fertility. Therefore, the bunny—especially the Easter Bunny—has become one of the best known symbols of spring in many countries.

## A Spring Tip for Preserving Creation

Did you know that the average person living in an industrialized country throws away almost three pounds of garbage every day? Most of this trash ends up in landfills.

A landfill is a huge pit dug into the ground. Garbage is dumped in, then a layer of dirt is spread over it. The dirt is supposed to cause the trash to decompose, breaking it down into minerals that go back into the soil.

When a landfill is full, grass and trees can be planted in the dirt on top. There are now public parks where many landfills used to be.

But two major problems are keeping a lot of landfills from doing what they are supposed to do:

Layers of garbage are being dumped into landfills faster than the previous layers of trash can decompose.

A lot of the garbage in landfills doesn't decompose at all. Some materials—such as glass—may lie in landfills for thousands of years. Other materials—such as plastics and metals—actually poison the soil.

How can you help? You can recycle. Most of the paper, glass, metal, and plastic that takes up space in landfills can be recycled. Newspapers, for instance, can be treated and reformed so they can be used again. Glass containers can be melted and made into new glass containers. Aluminum cans can be melted down and reshaped into almost anything. Plastic milk jugs can be heated and reformed into plastic toys, among other things.

So before you throw something away, stop to think for a minute. Could it be used again? Could it be made into something different, instead of clogging up a landfill for hundreds, maybe even thousands, of years? Maybe it could be recycled!

To set up your own recycling system, obtain four large boxes. Label one box "paper," another "glass," and the others "metal" and "plastic." Instead of throwing an aluminum can away, toss it into your "metal" box. Do the same with your paper, glass, and plastic. When the boxes begin to get full, take them to the recycling center nearest you. (To locate a recycling center, you may need to look in a telephone directory under "Recycling." If you can't find a center in the directory, ask your parents to contact the information agency of a local government office and ask them about the nearest center.) Some larger cities have recycling collection services.

You might even turn your recycling project into a money-making venture! Many recycling centers will pay for the materials you bring to them.

## Chapter 3
# Spring Is For. . .

### Growing Morning Glories

Morning glories are easy flowers to grow from seeds. If planted in the spring, they will produce flowers from early summer all the way through autumn. Their flowers are funnel-shaped and grow in clusters. When they first bloom in the early summer, they are usually bright blue. Later in the year, the blooms of most morning glories turn purplish.

Why are they called "morning glories"? Because they bloom with the first sign of light in the morning. The bloom gradually closes as the day wears on. By the time it gets dark, the flower is closed for the night.

Each morning glory bud blooms into a flower only once, and it blooms for only one day. But that's okay. A morning glory plant can produce lots of buds every day.

### Seed Starters

To grow morning glories, you first need seeds. You can get seeds in packages at a garden store. While you are there, also buy some potting soil.

When you get the seeds and soil home, take a close look at the soil. Notice how black it is. That means it's rich in minerals and nutrients that make plants grow. See those white specks in it? Those are little beads of fertilizer that, when combined with water, give plants a healthy start.

To make a place for your seeds to grow, remove the lid from an empty egg carton (or use twelve empty yogurt cups). Next, put a handful of potting soil in each of the twelve cups of the egg carton, and level the dirt off so that it's even across the top. Drop a seed in the middle of each cup. Push the seed about one-fourth of an inch (6 mm) into the soil, and then cover it with dirt. Keep the egg carton in a warm and sunny place.

Moisten each cup every day. A few drops of water will be fine. Too much will drown the seed and keep it from sprouting.

In a week or two, you should see a morning glory plant breaking the surface of the soil. Leave the plants in the egg carton until they grow two inches high. Then move each plant—soil and all—into a flower pot that has potting soil up to about one inch from the rim. You can put as many as three or four plants in a pot. Set the flower pots outside on warm sunny days. Move them inside if there is a chance of frost or a hard rain. (Don't forget to continue moistening the plants with a few drops of water every day.)

When the possibility of frost has passed, you will be ready to transplant your morning glories to a place where they will grow for the rest of the spring, summer, and even autumn.

### Transplanting

Picking a place for morning glories to grow is not easy. Morning glories are climbing plants that need to grow around or through things. So you may want to plant your morning glories around a tree or mailbox. As the vines grow, gently wrap them around the tree trunk or a post. If you are lucky enough to have a trellis in your yard, you can plant your morning glories at the foot of it. As the vines grow, gently weave them through some of the holes in the trellis. After a few weeks, the vines will grow through the trellis all by themselves.

To transplant your morning glories, simply dig a shallow hole, three or four inches deep. Choose a place where they will get lots of hours of sunlight each day. Reach into the flower pot and carefully remove the vine, its roots, and the soil around its roots. Put the plant and several handfuls of potting soil into the hole. Cover the hole with dirt so that it is level with the ground around it. (It is best to plant morning glories about two or three inches apart from each other. Then they will grow together, wrapping themselves around each other and giving their leaves a full look.)

Check on your morning glories daily to see how they are growing. After that, stand back and enjoy!

## WANT TO GROW ANOTHER KIND OF FLOWER?

If you'd like to grow another kind of flower, just follow the instructions given in the "Seed Starters" section. At a garden store, you'll find a big selection of different types of flower seeds. Choose your favorites, and help them to get started in some potting soil.

When your flowers are ready to be moved out of doors for the remainder of spring and summer, pick a place to plant them that is best for that particular kind of flower. The seed packet should provide information about your flower's ideal light and water conditions. Of course, you may want to buy a plant and flower guidebook. These books describe the best places to plant certain flowers, how much sunlight and water they need, and in what parts of the world they grow best.

### Sprouting a Garbage Can Garden

Take a peek inside your garbage can. All kinds of stuff, especially garbage from the kitchen, may have been thrown away. But did you know that you might have many of the ingredients you need for starting a garden right there in your trash? It's true!

Inside your garbage can you may find apple cores; carrot, turnip, or parsnip tops; old potatoes; and peach or plum pits—a lot of things that used to be part of a fruit or vegetable. These are the kinds of things you can use to start your own garden.

First, dig through the trash looking for the

Some of your seeds and pits may have difficulty sprouting. If so, chances are they need a winter to harden their outer coating. (Apple, peach, and plum seeds and pits often need cold weather to help them sprout properly.) You can wait until winter and leave your seeds outside, or you can put your seeds somewhere in your house that feels like winter.

The refrigerator? Good idea!

Put some of your seeds and pits in a jar. Then place the jar on its side in the refrigerator.

Once a week, turn the jar so the seeds and pits change positions. Leave it in the refrigerator for about six weeks. Your seeds will think they have experienced winter and will be ready to sprout.

thrown-away parts of fruits and vegetables. Too disgusting? You'd rather kiss snails? Okay. Ask your mom or dad to save the pieces of fruits and vegetables that are usually thrown away. Among the things you are especially looking for are fruit seeds and pits, the tops of root vegetables, and potatoes that have begun to sprout.

### In the Pits (and Seeds)

Collect seeds from apple cores, pears, grapes, or oranges, or the pits from peaches or plums. Place them in a bowl, and soak them in water overnight.

Borrow a shallow pan from the kitchen, and spread a layer of pebbles across the bottom of the pan. Pour in some potting soil and level it out across the pan. (The soil should be at least an inch-and-a-half (4 cm) deep, but no more than three inches (72 cm) deep.)

After soaking your seeds, plant them one-half inch deep in the soil. Be sure the seeds are at least an inch apart from each other. If you are using more than one kind of seed, plant seeds from the same kind of fruit together. Leave plenty of space between seeds from different fruits.

Moisten the soil, and then put the pan into a clear plastic bag. This helps the soil retain moisture. A bread wrapper will do for a bag—as long as it is clear enough to allow some sunlight through. Set the bag near a window so the soil and seeds can get plenty of sunlight.

In about a week, your seeds should sprout and you'll be able to see seedlings breaking the surface of the soil. Leave your sprouts in the pan until they grow an inch high. Then move the sprouts into a flower pot that has potting soil up to one inch from the rim. Do not put more than two plants in a pot. And if you do place two seedlings in a pot, be sure they are the same kind of plants—put an orange sprout with another orange sprout and a peach sprout with another peach sprout.

By late summer or early autumn, it will be time to remove these seedlings from the flower pots and plant them outdoors. Although it might sound wonderful to step outside and pluck a juicy peach, keep in mind that many fruit trees and vines can grow only in certain climates. Orange trees, for example, grow best in warmer areas. Apple trees, on the other hand, grow well in many climates.

### Upside-down Root Garden

Root vegetables are vegetables that grow beneath the ground's surface, like carrots, parsnips, onions, potatoes, and turnips. Even though the vegetable grows underground, the foliage—the green leaves—of the plant grows above ground.

So what would happen if you tried to grow the foliage of a root vegetable upside-down? Do you want to try?

Choose the type of root foliage garden you want to have. Carrots make nice foliage. So do parsnips, rutabagas (sometimes called swede turnips), and turnips. Collect six stems of your favorite root vegetable.

Slice away all but two inches of the vegetable, saving the stem part on top.

Use a knife to carve a hole into the root. Scoop out the center. (This hole should be able to hold water when the root is turned upside-down.)

Stick three toothpicks deep into the root—around the circle of the root as if to form a triangle.

Tie a string to each toothpick. (Be sure to tie the strings tight and into a double knot.)

Then, tie the three stings together at top.

Hang the root from a curtain rod above a window. It is best to hang the root in front of a window through which a lot of sunlight passes. (Or perhaps you will want to hang it outside, maybe from a porch or balcony.) Make sure there is always water in the hole that you carved into the root.

Follow these same instructions for your other five root vegetables.

Watch your upside-down garden grow!

As time passes, notice that the foliage does not grow straight down from the root. It grows out of the bottom of the root and then bends around the root back up toward the sky and sunlight. That's because the foliage is attracted to light and needs the sunlight to grow.

### Those Taters Have Eyes!

Every potato has spots on its skin from which sprouts can grow. These spots are called "eyes." To get a potato's eyes to sprout, cut a potato in half. Push the flat ends of the potato halves into a bowl of wet sand. Cover the top of the bowl, and put it in a dark place—the back of a cupboard will work just fine. Check on the potato halves every few days. When the eyes have sprouted, take the cover off the bowl and put the sprouts in a sunny place. Give the sprouts two more weeks to grow in the bowl, and then transplant them into a flower pot. Better yet, find a good garden spot outdoors and plant the potato—flat side down. Leave about an inch of the sprouts above ground. Before long, you'll have your own little potato patch!

### Start a Guacamole Factory

Guacamole is a green spread made from mashed avocados, tomatoes, mayonnaise and seasonings. It's delicious on tacos and other Mexican foods. To start your own guacamole factory, start with the avocados.

Buy an avocado, cut it in half, and remove the pit from the middle. Stick toothpicks into both sides of the pit. Fill a small glass with water, and balance the pit on a glass. The pointed end of the pit should be up—out of the water. Make sure the bottom of the pit is barely touching the water.

Put the glass in a sunny place. After three or four weeks, a root should start sprouting out of the bottom of the pit. When that root is two inches (5 cm) long, remove the pit from the glass, take out the toothpicks, and plant the seed in a flower pot filled with potting soil.

Wait! Don't put the pit all the way under the dirt. Just make sure the root and half of the pit are beneath the surface. Keep the dirt moist, and keep the pot in a sunny place. Soon, the top part of the pit will split open, and a green stem will grow out of it. In time, leaves will grow off the stem. Then you can claim to be starting your own guacamole factory.

## Making an Anemometer

An anemometer is an instrument that measures the speed of wind. People who study weather—meteorologists—use technical anemometers to measure the speed of wind in miles per hour or kilometers per hour.

You can make an anemometer of your own. Of course, it won't be as sophisticated as the kind meteorologists use. It won't tell you the exact speed of the wind, but it will tell you how strong the wind is on different days, and at different times and places.

To make your own anemometer, you'll need:

*a hammer and a four-inch (10 cm) nail*
*a wooden board about five inches (12 cm) square*
    *and one inch (22 cm) thick*
*corrugated cardboard about five inches (12 cm) square*
    *(this can be cut from a cardboard box)*
*a plastic drinking straw*
*masking tape*
*a stapler*
*four small paper cups*
*a pen*

Use the hammer to drive a nail straight through the center of the wooden board. Turn the board over, then pick up the square of cardboard. Very carefully push the cardboard square onto the nail, punching a hole into the center of the cardboard. Then take the cardboard off the nail and set it aside for a few seconds.

Slide the plastic straw over the nail in the wooden board. Then push the cardboard over the straw so that the straw comes up about a quarter of an inch through the hole in the cardboard. (Be careful not to bend or break the straw!) Using tape, secure the straw to the cardboard square.

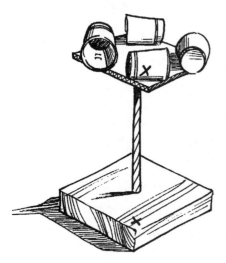

Then staple the paper cups to each of the four corners of the cardboard square. Be sure that the mouth of each cup is facing the bottom of the cup in front of it. When you're done, align the cardboard square evenly with the wooden board below it, and mark an X on one cup and on the corresponding corner of the wooden board below it.

Now your anemometer is ready to use!

To use your anemometer, set it down in the places where you want to measure wind speed. Your anemometer will not tell you how fast the wind is blowing in miles per hour, but it will tell you how fast it is blowing in revolutions per minute (RPMs).

To determine the RPMs of the wind on your anemometer, check the second-hand on your watch. Plan to look back to your watch in about thirty seconds. Count the times that the X-cup passes the X on the wooden board. After thirty seconds, multiply the number of passes by two. The answer will equal the number of RPMs in that place. (If looking back and forth starts to make you cross-eyed, ask a friend to help. One of you can watch the clock while the other one counts the revolutions of the anemometer.)

Test the RPMs in different places and on different days. You may even want to keep a record of how many RPMs the wind was blowing at a certain time: just before a storm, on your birthday, when you're flying a kite—or when your kite won't fly.

# Chapter 4
# Summer Stuff

## Reason for the Season

There's no doubt about it. It's getting hotter! The sun seems to shine its hot light on you whenever you are outdoors. In fact, the sun is still shining far into the evening. There is a whole lot more daylight and a whole lot less nighttime. What's going on here?

What's going on is summer.

Ever since the first day of spring on March 21, the earth has been tilting more and more toward the sun. That has made the weather start to get warmer in the Northern Hemisphere. Finally, the North Pole leans toward the sun as much as it ever will in the course of a year. That day—June 21—is known as the summer solstice, and it marks the first day of summer. On that day, there are more hours of daylight than on any other day of the year. (Of course, that also means there are fewer hours of darkness than on any other day of the year.)

After June 21, the earth tilts more and more away from the sun. The days gradually get shorter and the nights gradually get longer. So why do the days usually get hotter after June 21?

It gets hotter after the summer solstice because it takes time for the sun's light to heat up the earth's surface. The fact is it is the heat released by the earth's surface that determines how hot the air is, not how close the planet is to the sun. And the earth's surface sometimes doesn't reach it highest temperature until a month or so after June 21. That's why the hottest days of summer usually come sometime in July or August.

## Send in the Clouds

Did you ever lie on your back in the warm summer grass and look up at the clouds? Did you see the shapes of faces or animals in some of the clouds? Next time you're looking up at the clouds, maybe you'd like to know a little more about how they're made and what effect they have on the weather.

What makes a cloud?

The earth's surface is the first thing that is needed to make a cloud. Strange, but true. Without the warm moist air created by the earth's surface, there would be no clouds.

Clouds form when warm air rises and blends in with the cooler air above it. The warm air is moist and can hold water vapor. The cold air is dry and cannot hold water vapor very well.

When warm moist air meets cold dry air, the cold air can hold only so much water vapor. What it cannot hold is turned into tiny water droplets (closer to the earth) or ice crystals (farther away from the earth). When these droplets or crystals come together, they form clouds.

## Herbs for Herb

Meet Herb. Herb is not feeling well. His stomach is upset. So Herb's mother has gone to the drug store to pick up some things that will make Herb feel better. Most of the things she'll buy are made from herbs. Herbs are plants that grow close to the ground. They have juicy stems when they are young, and those stems turn into a hard, woody tissue when they get old. (It usually only takes one season of the year for them to start getting pretty old.) For most herbs, the part that grows above the ground dies every year, but the roots stay alive and produce new plants each year. Summer is the best time to find most herbs.

But back to Herb and the herbs. Frankly, even Herb's mother doesn't realize that herbs are in most of the things she is buying to make her son feel better. The stomach medicine, for instance, is made from the roots of the yellow gentian—one type of herb. And the tablets she bought for Herb's dizziness include powdered ginseng—made from another herb.

Vanilla ice cream, Herb's favorite sick-day treat, is flavored with the herb called vanilla. And the herb that makes Herb's soup taste so good is basil. Of course, Herb likes to drink tea with his soup. The tea that Herb drinks as he eats his soup is balm tea, made from yet another herb. The candy that Herb can have only after eating all of his soup is flavored with mint, peppermint, and spearmint. All herbs.

While Herb's mother is at the drugstore, she picks up a few things for herself. First she buys a bottle of perfume, one that relies on the herb lavender for some of its scent. She buys some soap that contains marjoram, another herb.

Later that day, Herb has taken his medicine and is eating his soup and drinking his tea. He's already feeling better. He feels so much better that he's looking forward to ice cream and candy.

Thanks in part to herbs, Herb will soon be back outside playing in the summer sunshine again. And maybe, when he's through, he'll spend some time looking for herbs—the plants that have spiced up his life.

## Summer Bugs Me

When warm weather arrives, insects seem to appear out of nowhere. One moment, the air is clear and the ground is empty. The next minute, creatures of every sort are flying through the air and crawling on the ground. In summer, insects seem to be everywhere.

They practically are. Scientists know of almost a million different kinds of insects—small, six-legged animals. And as many as ten thousand new types of insects are discovered every year. Some scientists think that there are another ten million kinds of insects that have not yet been discovered. Don't get too upset, though. Most insects are rarely ever seen and cause no harm to anyone or anything. In fact, all of them have an important part to play in creation.

### The Good

Ladybird beetles, also know as ladybugs, are both pretty and good. Their red backs and wings with black spots make them pretty. The fact that they eat insects that destroy plants makes them good. Ladybugs are so good that fruit farmers actually buy them and set them free in their orchards. Many gardeners do the same at home.

## DON'T TOUCH THAT WEED!

Most weeds that grow in the summer are harmless. But some can make your summer miserable. Poison ivy, poison oak, and poison sumac can give you an itchy rash.

These weeds have invisible oils on their leaves. When these oils come into contact with skin, they react to the oils already in your skin, causing red, itchy bumps to crop up. These oils can last a long time too. If the oils get on your clothes—or somebody else's clothes, for that matter—and later come into contact with your skin, they can still cause an allergic rash. You can even pick up the oils of these weeds from the fur of a dog or a cat.

So avoid these weeds if at all possible. If you should mistakenly touch their leaves, wash with soap and water as soon as you can. Wash your clothes quickly too!

Bees might seem bad because they can sting us. But they really provide a great service. By flying from flower to flower, they help flowers, fruits, and vegetables to pollinate. And bees, by sipping the nectar out of flowers and placing it in combs inside their hives, create honey.

### The Bad

Boll weevils eat and destroy cotton plants. Moths and carpet beetles sneak into our houses and eat through clothing, carpeting, and upholstery. Termites and woodworms (or furniture beetles) eat the wooden beams and floors of buildings, often weakening them and making them unsafe. Mosquitoes, ticks, and other bloodsucking insects can carry such diseases as malaria and African sleeping sickness in some tropical countries.

### The Pretty

Fireflies, also called "lightning bugs," are actually beetles. Through a chemical reaction they trigger in their bodies, male fireflies can flash light. Female fireflies cannot fly because they have such short wings. So, the males fly around blinking their little lights in an attempt to find a mate! Even with their large, bulging eyes, dragonflies are considered pretty because of the multicolored designs on their wings, and the way they catch and reflect the sun as they hover in mid-air. Of course, among the most beautiful of all insects are butterflies. They fly gracefully, displaying an incredible variety of colors and sizes and wingspans. Butterflies are also good, helping to pollinate flowers like bees do.

### The Ugly

The Goliath beetle is both big and ugly. It has claws at the end of its hairy legs and a strange-looking head with what appear to be four sets of eyes. And these monsters can grow to be four inches long! The giant water beetle can grow to be almost two-and-a-half inches

long. And when they go scampering across the floor as an unwelcome guest in your house, they are definitely ugly. The stag beetle, with its sticky legs and pincher mouth, is not at all attractive—especially when it clings to your clothing while you're playing outside.

Whether good or bad, pretty or ugly, all bugs were created for a purpose. Many provide food for hungry birds and animals. Some feed on dead plants and animals, adding rich minerals and nutrients to the soil. Chances are, you won't fall in love with a Goliath beetle. But it would probably think you're pretty strange too—and look how special you are!

This summer, see if you can discover some insects that you've never seen before. Most insects aren't that hard to find if you look closely enough. You may even want to buy an insect guidebook to help you with your discoveries. A guidebook will give an up-close look at a wide variety of bugs and may also tell you more about each insect's role in the world.

## SOME SUNNY FACTS

The sun is the center of our solar system. Without it, life couldn't exist on earth. All forms of life depend on it for heat, light, and energy. But, of course, it's summer—you probably know how good sunshine is. Here are some amazing facts about the sun that you might not know:

The sun. . .

is only one of billions of stars in the universe.

is about ninety-three million miles away from the earth.

projects light across the solar system. It takes that light about eight minutes and twenty seconds to reach the earth.

is 865,000 miles wide (or about 109 times bigger than the earth).

is thought to be about ten thousand degrees (Fahrenheit) at its surface, and perhaps twenty-seven million degrees at its center.

is about 75% hydrogen, about 24% helium. At least 70 other elements make up the last 1%.

# Chapter 5
# Summer Fun!

## Weather Poetry

Predicting the weather is a tough business, even now that we have weather satellites, technical computers, and weather balloons to help us. So imagine how hard it must have been for people to guess the weather before they had any scientific equipment.

And yet, people living long ago were still able to predict the weather with a fair amount of accuracy. How? Over time they learned that certain patterns in nature could help them know what to expect.

For instance, someone noticed that almost every time ants built up the sides of their hills, it rained. That person told someone else, who told someone else. Pretty soon, lots of people were checking ant hills to see if it was going to rain. A lot of times, the ants were right!

Sailors and shepherds used to watch the skies closely for signs of changes in the weather. When the setting sun caused a red glow in the western sky, they could look forward to sunny and pleasant weather the next day. But if the rising sun caused a red glow in the eastern sky, they should prepare for storms.

In time, people put their weather predictions into a rhyme:

*Red sky at night, sailor's (shepherd's) delight;*
*Red sky in the morning, sailors (shepherds) take warning!*

Believe it or not, they were right! A red sky in the evening is caused by the sun shining through dry, dusty air. Rain rarely develops from this kind of air. On the other hand, a red sky in the morning is caused by sunlight shining through moist, humid air. This type of air usually develops into rain—sometimes even violent storms—in less than nine hours.

Farmers, too, had ways of predicting the weather. They figured out that they could expect rain when insect-eating birds flew close to the ground. The farmers too put their weather prediction into a rhyme:

*Swallows flying low and near to the ground*
*Means that soon a storm of rain will be found.*

The farmers were right too! When the heavier cool air falls toward the earth's surface, it carries a lot of insects with it. To eat the insects, swallows fly low to the ground.

The cool air forces the warm air up and away from the surface of the earth, which often causes rain clouds to form.

Not all weather rhymes have proved to be right, however. Take this one for instance:

*A ring around the moon*
*Means rain is coming soon.*

Meteorologists have found that the hazy ring around the moon is caused by the moonlight shining through clouds that are full of ice crystals. When the clouds are high, the ring is small. When the clouds are low, the ring is large. Regardless of the size of the ring, however, weather scientists have determined that rings around the moon are unreliable for predicting rainy weather.

## All About Ants

No summer picnic would be complete without ants. They love to eat outdoors—especially when others supply all the food! But ants are much more than just unwelcome dinner guests. In fact, entomologists—scientists who study insects—say that ants may be the most highly developed of all insects. Why? Because most ants live in colonies. An ant colony is one large nest providing a home for sometimes thousands—even millions—of ants.

You probably know about the ants that build their colonies in underground tunnels. And you probably know that some ants build tall mounds of dirt for their colonies. But did you know that some ants live inside trees and hollow parts of plants? Or that some ants build their colonies by weaving a leaf together?

### Classy Ants

In most colonies, the ants are members of a caste—or a social class or group—that they are born into. That means as soon as they emerge from their eggs, or pupa, they carry out specific duties. There are three castes of ants.

*Caste One: the queen.* The queen has two jobs—to begin a colony and then to lay eggs for the rest of her life. After she finds a place for a colony, she hardly ever leaves the nest. She begins laying what will eventually be thousands of eggs. Most of the eggs will produce worker ants. These ants leave the colony and bring the queen food. Once she feels the worker ants have her colony in good working order, she lays eggs that will produce new queen ants and male ants.

*Caste Two: the worker.* Worker ants are also females. The job of some workers is nothing more than keeping the queen well-fed. Other workers repair the colony and sometimes make it bigger. Others defend the colony from enemies. Others care for the young ants, and still others gather food. Usually, the workers are assigned just one job all of their lives.

*Caste Three: the male ant.* Male ants rarely work or live in the colony. Their life spans are much shorter than that of females. Their only job is to mate with the queen.

When the queen and the male ants reach adulthood, they have wings. While flying far above the ground, the males mate with the queen. All the eggs the queen will lay throughout her life are the result of this one mating flight.

After mating, the ants return to the ground. The queen rips off her wings—never to fly again—and begins to search for a place to build the colony. The male ants wander away and die.

### An Ant Colony: The Inside Story

Even though there is usually only one entrance to an ant colony, inside is a

**43**

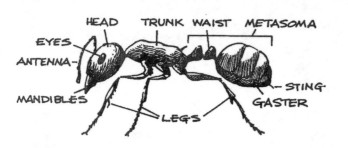

HEAD TRUNK WAIST METASOMA
EYES
ANTENNA
MANDIBLES
LEGS
STING
GASTER

# ANTS ON THE ATTACK

Although they are small, ants aren't defenseless when they're attacked. Some ants bite, while others sting.

About half of all types of ants have stingers. (Because of their shape and the fact that many of them have stingers, some entomologists think ants used to be a kind of wasp. Over time, these scientists say, they developed into their own species of insect.) Both fire ants and bulldog ants have stingers strong enough to pierce a person's skin.

Most ants release a small dosage of painful poison when they sting. Fire ants, in the southeastern United States, can, in large numbers, inflict great pain on humans. To a human, an ant sting usually hurts for only a few seconds. But the poison is powerful enough to drive other insects away.

Those ants that cannot sting can always bite. Their mandibles—the mouth and jaw—are usually very strong. When an ant bites a human, it can hurt for several seconds. But that same bite can be deadly to an ant from another colony.

Ants are especially fierce fighters when defending their home from invaders. Sometimes several ants will lock their jaws on an invading ant's antennae and legs, stretching out the invader's body. The other ants move in, using their mandibles to crush and tear the enemy apart.

vast collection of rooms that serve many purposes. The biggest room is typically the queen's chamber. Here the queen lays her eggs. Worker ants are allowed into the queen's chamber to bring her food and to pick up her eggs.

When workers pick up the eggs, they carry them to other rooms known as nurseries, where the workers care for the eggs until young ants emerge.

In addition to the queen's chamber and nurseries, there are "lounges" where worker ants may gather to rest, and storerooms for the supplies of seeds and other food gathered by the ants.

In winter, the ants crawl down to the warmest rooms in the colony, deep below the surface of the ground.

## The Night Thistles Saved a Castle

Thistles aren't the prettiest of flowers. Their long green stems are full of sharp needles. The flower at the top of the stem looks like a little ball with porcupine-like pins all the way around. Shooting out from the top of the ball are hundreds of red prickly needles. All in all, the thistle looks like a mean wild weed that is still trying to become a flower.

Even so, the thistle is the national flower of Scotland. The Scots generally agree that there are many prettier flowers, but still they treasure the thistle. An event that happened more than a thousand years ago is the reason why.

At that time, fierce warriors known as Vikings were invading Europe. The Vikings often attacked towns and castles, sometimes killing all the people, stealing their food and treasures, and burning everything down. They were so vicious that people were terrified of them coming to their town.

One summer night, the Vikings landed on the banks of the River Clyde and decided to attack the castle of Scotland's king. They quietly surrounded the castle—so quietly that they did not even awaken the king and his soldiers who were asleep inside.

A moat surrounded the castle. But moats didn't bother the Vikings. They knew that by taking off their sandals and wading across the moat, they could still reach the castle and attack.

On their leader's signal, the Vikings took off their sandals and quietly rushed into the moat. But they weren't quiet for long.

Because the summer had been so hot and dry, the moat had dried up. Instead of being full of water, it was filled with thousands of sharp, prickly thistles!

When the barefoot Vikings stepped on the thistles, they screamed out in pain. When some of them tried to turn around and run out of the moat, the Vikings behind them pushed them so that they fell down onto the thistles, screaming even louder.

All the yelling and commotion woke the king and his soldiers, who immediately launched an attack on the Vikings. The Vikings—who were still howling over their injured feet, legs, backs, and necks—were hurting too much to defend themselves. The king defeated the Vikings

that night, driving them back to their ships and away from Scotland.

And that is why the people of Scotland, even today, proudly claim the lowly thistle as the national flower.

## Thanking a Tree

Next time you take a deep breath, be sure to thank a tree. Trees and other plants that grow green leaves take bad gases like carbon dioxide out of the air. They turn those bad gases into food for themselves and then release oxygen into the air.

Oxygen is the most important gas for humans and animals. Without it, we couldn't live. Every person and animal takes oxygen out of the air as they breathe. If it weren't for trees and plants, we would soon use up all the available oxygen and die. But we don't have to worry about breathing as long as there are plenty of trees and green plants around. Every second of every day a leaf-growing plant is helping us breathe by pushing fresh oxygen into our air.

Thank a tree when you think about breathing. And maybe even lend the earth—and yourself—a helping hand by planting another tree sometime this summer.

## The History of a Tree

Do you live near woods or a forest? If you do, you may stumble upon a fallen tree trunk as you take a summer walk. Before that tree was chopped, blown, or knocked down, it probably lived many years. The story behind those years is written inside a tree's trunk.

When you find a tree stump, stop and examine the top of it. See all the rings inside? Those are called annual rings. Every ring indicates one year of that tree's life. Count all the rings from the center to the

## TREES ARE COOL—AND TASTY TOO!

Trees do more than turn carbon dioxide into oxygen. They help us and our environment in these ways too. Trees help us to conserve energy. Trees planted in the right places around your home can reduce your need for air conditioning, which uses up a lot of electricity. Trees can make cities a cooler place to live in the summer. Concrete, asphalt, and other street and building materials absorb sunlight and release heat. The more trees there are in a city, the less direct sunlight the streets and buildings can absorb. That means they'll release less heat. By planting trees in the right places in your city or town, you can help to make your hometown a cooler place to live and visit in the summertime. And, of course, some trees give us tasty and healthy fruits and nuts to eat!

bark. If there are forty rings, then the tree was forty years old when it was cut down. If there are seventy rings, then the tree was seventy. But don't stop once you're done counting. You can learn a lot more about a tree's life by looking closely at its rings.

For example, does the tree have very narrow rings in the center? If it does, then the tree is telling you that during the first years of its life, it may have lived in the shadow of bigger trees. When a young tree, a sapling, lives in the shadow of bigger trees, it doesn't get as much sunlight and rainfall. Thus, it doesn't grow very fast. Narrow rings tell you that the tree grew slowly.

Wider rings mean that the tree grew quickly. Usually trees grow faster in the later years of their lives than they do during their first years. That's because as the tree gets bigger, it's able to claim more sunlight and rainfall for itself. So, it grows faster. For that reason, wider rings are usually in the outer part of the trunk.

Are there places where the rings of the tree are indented—making a V? If so, it's probably a good indication that a branch grew out of the trunk at that place in the tree. If the V begins on the sixteenth ring from the center, then the branch began growing out of the tree trunk when the tree was sixteen years old.

Is there a dark, black scar somewhere in the rings of the tree? If there is, the tree may be telling you about a time when it was damaged by fire. The scar can also tell you how old the tree was when it was burned. Look closely at the rings around the scar. Are they narrower than most? The fire probably slowed the tree's growth for a year or two.

As you examine the history of a tree, perhaps you will want to do something the tree could not do—write its story down on paper. After closely looking at its rings, write a story about what you think happened to the tree during each year of its life.

## Tips for Saving Trees

How would you like to save some trees from unnecessary destruction? It isn't as hard as you might think.

You can save trees by saving paper. Many trees are turned into wood pulp, which is used to make paper. Of course, you don't have to stop using paper altogether. But almost everyone agrees that it would help the earth a lot if we used less paper—and used it more than once. Here are some ideas:

Instead of wrapping birthday presents in fancy paper, use the comics from your Sunday newspaper. They are colorful, and they might even get a smile out of the person who's getting the present.

"How does that help trees?" you might ask.

Once store-bought wrapping paper is torn off the gifts, it is thrown away. Then, it's hauled off to a landfill, where it takes years to decompose, due to the chemicals used to manufacture it.

The comic pages of a newspaper are made with paper that can be recycled easily. So after your friends or family members unwrap their presents from you, just stack the wrapping paper (the comics) with other newspapers. When the stack is a foot or so high, ask your parents to help you take it to a recycling center.

That way, you will have used the paper at least three times:

1. Paper is used to produce the comics.
2. Paper is used to wrap presents.
3. Paper is recycled for some other purpose.

Use fewer paper towels. Better yet, stop using paper towels at all. Paper towels are used only once—to wipe your hands or clean up a spill. Why not use a cloth towel instead? A cloth towel can wipe your hands and clean up a spill. Then the towel can be washed and used again and again and again. In the long run, cloth towels will cost less money than paper towels. By using cloth instead of paper for several years, you'll save a whole lot of trees!

Write to the companies that send you catalogs or mail you don't really want, and nicely ask them to stop. (Maybe even encourage your parents and friends to do the same.) Most catalogs are printed on paper that cannot be recycled, and few companies use recycled paper for their catalogs. Therefore, most catalogs end up in a landfill. Hint: To send your letter to the catalog company, use the reply envelope that's inside most catalogs. You'll save paper—and trees—and you'll be sure to get the address right.

If you don't usually use both sides of a sheet of notebook paper, start doing so. Your paper will go twice as far!

Buy—and encourage your parents to buy—paper products that have been recycled. Most such products have a special symbol somewhere on the label. It's a triangle made up of three green arrows.

# Chapter 6
# Summer Is For . . .

### Composting Versus the Landfill

The amount of trash produced by the average person puts a great strain on the earth's environment. In some places in the world—like Great Britain, the United States, and Canada—each person throws away as much as four pounds (20 kg) of trash every day. Because trash doesn't have time to decompose in landfills before more trash is piled onto it, landfills quickly fill up. Soon we will run out of places to dump our garbage.

Instead of throwing away all your trash, you could compost some of it. Composting turns some of your garbage into fertilizer for plants.

This summer, try an experiment to find out which is the best way to dispose of trash—composting or landfill dumping. To get started, you'll need to build your own homemade landfill and your own homemade compost heap.

### Building a Landfill

To build your own miniature landfill, start with an empty, clear plastic two-liter soft-drink bottle. Use a utility knife to carefully cut off the top part of the bottle (the spout).

Fill the bottom third of the bottle with

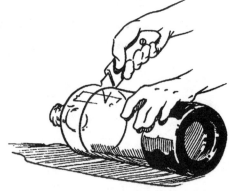

soil. Then dump your first items of trash into the landfill: two facial tissues, a plastic soft-drink bottle cap, a piece of cooked potato, and the leftovers from a sack lunch—including a piece of the sack. Put another layer of dirt on top of the trash so that the bottle is about two-thirds full.

Add a second layer of trash to the miniature landfill: a wadded-up piece of aluminum foil, a polystyrene cup, a banana skin, and a piece of cardboard cut from a cereal box.

Finally, press the contents of the bottle down with your hand and fill the rest of the bottle with dirt (up to an inch (22 cm) from the rim). Sprinkle the surface of your miniature landfill with water every other day.

Take a look at the trash inside your miniature landfill every time you sprinkle the surface. Note any changes you see taking place.

## Building a Compost Heap

To build your own compost heap, you will need a plastic garbage can with a lid. (The size of the container is up to you.) Use a utility knife to carefully punch about forty small holes in the lid of the garbage can. The holes should be big enough to allow plenty of air into the can but not big enough to allow flies in.

Fill the bottom of the can with dirt. Then dump in some vegetable leftovers. Pieces of cooked potato, fruit peelings, even bread crusts and cereal bits will work well. You may also want to add some decaying leaves. (You can speed up the composting process by cutting all these things into small pieces before dumping them into the can.) As you begin your compost heap, be sure there is only as much trash as there is dirt.

Next, to build a good compost heap you're going to need some help from a few of your creepy, crawly friends. Worms, sow bugs, pill bugs, and springtails will probably be your best helpers. These soil animals

If you don't live near a bait and tackle shop—but do live in the United States (or can receive US mail)—you might like to get a free brochure and order form from a company specializing in worm composting. Write to:

Mary Applehof
Flowerfield Enterprises
10332 Shaver Road
Kalamazoo, Michigan 49002

Mary Applehof is the author of *Worms Eat My Garbage*, a book about worm composting, available at the above address for $10.45 (ask about the shipping costs if you live outside the United States).

are recyclers that will eat parts of the trash and turn it into minerals that will enrich the soil. Of course, you don't have to dig up your yard to find some of these crawly creatures. The best place to get them is at a bait and tackle shop—a place where fishing supplies are sold. If the shop doesn't have some of the creatures you want, ask the shop manager to order them for you.

Use a strong, firm stick to stir the compost for several minutes. The mixture in the can should be moist, but not wet. If it feels too dry as you stir, sprinkle some water into the can and stir it some more. If it feels too wet, sprinkle some sawdust or dry dirt into the can and continue stirring.

A word of warning: Meat and bones can make good compost, but they attract rats. Unless you want to chase rats away from your compost heap, it is best not to toss meat and bones into the compost can. Vegetable garbage, leaves, and grass clippings make the best compost.

Keep your compost can outdoors, of course! In hot summer weather, move the can into the shade. This will protect the soil animals inside the can that are helping you to compost. If the weather gets cold, move the can into the sunlight, which will warm the can's contents.

Every time you add more vegetable garbage, also add a little more dirt and stir the mixture. Note any changes you see or feel (when stirring) taking place.

When the can is three-quarters full or the mixture becomes too deep and too thick for you to stir, stop adding vegetable garbage. For three to six weeks more, let time, the weather, and your soil animals do the rest of the work for you.

In less than two months from the last time you added vegetable garbage, you will have compost. Spread several handfuls of compost around your favorite trees, flowers, garden plants, and house plants—and watch them grow!

## And the Winner Is . . .

When your experiment is finished, these are some of the things you will have learned about composting and landfills.

Some things—like plastic, aluminum foil, and polystyrene—take a long time, maybe even hundreds or thousands of years, to break down and decompose. These items will still be taking up space in landfills many years from now. Paper and cardboard break down and decompose faster than some other materials. (But why clog up landfills even for a short time with paper that can be recycled?)

Vegetable garbage takes a long time to break down and decompose by itself. Add soil, and vegetable garbage breaks down faster. Add moisture, and it breaks down even faster. Add worms and some stirring, however, and vegetable garbage will break down and become fertilizer in just a few months!

There are some things that even worms won't touch. Among them are plastic, aluminum foil, and polystyrene. If you had put these items in your compost heap, they would have remained intact even with the soil animals eating around them and you stirring them. They would never become minerals to enrich the soil in your lifetime—or even in many lifetimes!

What is created within nature or with natural ingredients—like potato pieces, fruit peelings, and bread crusts—nature has a way of disposing of and turning into something good. But much of what is manufactured—like plastic, foil, and polystyrene—cannot be handled by nature. We must find a better way of disposing of it—or better yet, a way to recycle it.

Maybe you'd like to take up making compost as a hobby. If you have two cans, you can start one compost heap while another is finishing. Perhaps you could even sell your compost to neighbors who want the best for their gardens. Natural compost can be expensive to buy at garden shops. People who have gardens might be happy to pay you for a regular, small supply of compost.

So now is the time to declare a winner. Composting or another full landfill? Composting wins hands down!

## Bird Watching

More birds live in your area during the summer than any other time of the year. So there's no better time for bird watching. Providing food for them is one of the best ways to get birds near enough to watch them closely.

Pigeons and ducks that are city dwellers often rely on people for food. These birds don't mind coming within a few feet of people if those people are tossing out bread crumbs.

But what about other birds? Most birds will fly away if they sense a human being—or a cat or dog—nearby.

How can you lure a sparrow or a titmouse close enough to watch them?

One way is to watch them close-up from a distance—using field glasses or binoculars. Another way to watch birds close-up is to open your own window-feeder restaurant for birds.

## The Window Feeder Restaurant

To build a window feeder restaurant for birds, you will need a 1-foot (30 cm) square wooden board that is 2-inch (5 mm) thick. You'll also need a wooden post that is about 2 inches (2 cm) square and 6 feet (2 meters) long.

First, center the square piece of wood over one end of the post and nail it to the post. Choose a window through which you can watch the birds from indoors, and dig a hole 1-foot (30 cm) deep just outside that window. Place the post in the hole, and fill in the hole with dirt and rocks. Now you have a sturdy platform for your window feeder restaurant.

Buy some bird seed at your local grocery store, and sprinkle several handfuls of seed across the top of the platform. It may take several hours or even days before the birds discover the feeder, so be patient. Eventually, the birds will come—usually one at a time but sometimes in groups—to eat at your restaurant.

When they do, sit very still inside your home and watch. Even your slightest movements can scare the birds away. By having a bird restaurant, you'll not only learn how birds eat and what kinds of seeds they like, you may also have a chance to learn how they react to each other.

For instance, some birds, like jays, like to eat alone. They will rarely allow another bird at the restaurant while they are dining there. Finches, on the other hand, seem to like eating in groups. Don't be surprised to find four, five or even six finches dining at the same time.

Listen closely while watching the birds. Hear the chirps? Learn to identify the bird's song while looking at the bird. Then, later, you'll be able to tell what kind of bird is singing outside even when you can't see it.

Keep a good supply of bird seed on the board, and birds will visit your restaurant time and time again.

## BUT WHERE ARE THE ROBINS?

After you've had your restaurant open for a while, you may notice that no robins have stopped off to dine. The problem is the kind of food you're serving.

Not all birds are seed eaters. Many birds eat only insects or worms. Others, like owls, prefer rats, mice, lizards, and even other birds for their meals. Because birds such as owls, robins, bluebirds, and blackbirds like to catch and eat live prey, it's practically impossible for you to serve the kind of meal that would bring them close to your restaurant.

## Making Sun Tea

It's a hot, dry summer day. No doubt about it—you're thirsty. Water would be good. But tea would be even better.

If you had planned ahead, you could have taken advantage of the sun's rays and enjoyed a cool, refreshing glass of sun tea. It's really very simple.

Fill a clear, one-gallon (4 ltr) glass jug with water. Put three tea bags into the jug, seal it tightly with a lid, and set it outside where it can get direct sunlight. Leave the jug for several hours.

When the water inside the jug is as dark as you like your tea, take the jug inside. Pour yourself a glass of sun tea over ice, and quench your thirst!

## Making Water from Dirt

Imagine yourself stranded in the middle of an open field on a dry, hot summer day. With the sun beaming down on you, you realize you're going to need water to drink. And soon. But there's no water in sight. In fact, there may not be any water for miles around.

Did you know that if you had the right materials and enough time, you could use the sun to make a glass of water for yourself? It's true. In one day's time, you could have a drink of solar-generated water.

To make solar generated water at home, you'll need the following items:

*a shovel*
*a drinking glass*
*a sheet of plastic about eighteen inches (50 cm) square*
    *(you can cut this out of a plastic garbage bag)*
*a small stone*
*several large, flat rocks*

First, dig a one-foot square hole (one-foot (30 cm) wide, long, and deep) in the ground. (Be sure to ask for permission before you begin.) Pat down the sides of the hole to pack the soil together. Then put a glass in the center of the bottom of the hole.

Cover the hole with the sheet of plastic. Fasten down the edges of the sheet—tightly—by using several large, flat rocks. It is important that no air can flow into the hole while you are making solar generated water. Then drop a small stone in the middle of the plastic so that the plastic sheet sags directly over the glass.

Now all you have to do is wait.

When the sunlight causes heat to build up in the hole, the moisture in the soil begins to evaporate. In essence, the soil's moisture becomes like invisible steam. The plastic sheet over the hole prevents the steam from escaping into the air. Therefore, the moisture collects on the plastic sheet and begins to form water droplets.

These water droplets slide down the sagging sheet of plastic, and finally drip off into the glass. Depending on how brightly the sun is shining and how much moisture is in the ground, this method should

## DETECTION BY THE BOOK

If you really want to be a good tree detective, you need to buy yourself a good field guide. One of the best is *A Field Guide to Trees and Shrubs* by George A. Petrides. Sponsored by both the National Audubon Society and the National Wildlife Federation, this field guide is published by Houghton Mifflin Company in the United States.

Why bother with another book? There are simply too many varieties of trees to remember them all. With a field guide handy, you'll have all the information you'll need right at your fingertips.

This book has several pages of tree silhouettes that will help you identify some trees by their shapes. It also contains illustrations of almost seven hundred leaves from different trees and shrubs. It points out the different ways trees grow and where they grow best. There are even illustrations and descriptions of the flowers, fruits, and nuts some trees produce.

produce about a quart (1 liter) of solar generated fresh water a day. And, depending on where you live, the water you end up with is likely to be cleaner than the water from your kitchen tap!

## Becoming a Tree Detective

Summer is probably the best time of year to learn about the different kinds of trees. In the summer, each tree gives you several clues that can help you identify it, helping you to become a tree detective.

## On Pines and Needles

It's fun to learn to look for certain differences between trees. For instance, does the tree you're looking at have needle-like leaves? If so, you're probably looking at a type of evergreen tree. Most of these trees bear cones, so they are called conifers. Conifers include pines, firs, spruces, cedars, and larches. These trees bear needles that stay green all year round.

Pines usually have long, slender needles for leaves. Firs have fan-like branches with short, pointy needles emerging flat from the sides of each branch. Spruces, like firs, also have fan-like branches, but the short, pointy needles emerge from all the way around a branch. The needles of a cedar are shorter than those of a fir or spruce, but they're so thick on the branch that they are sometimes difficult to distinguish from each other.

## Trees That Shed

Perhaps the tree you are looking at has broad leaves. If so, then it's probably a deciduous tree. Deciduous trees bear broad, flat leaves late in the spring and early in the summer. These leaves stay green only until autumn, when they turn red, yellow, and orange and then fall to the ground.

Does the tree you're looking at have big leaves with rounded fingers? It could be an oak. Does it have medium-sized leaves with sharp, pointed fingers? Perhaps it is a maple. Are its leaves fan-shaped with tiny, pointed ridges around the edge. Maybe it's a poplar. (It could also be a beech, hickory, birch, or an elm!)

Identifying deciduous trees only by their leaves can be difficult. And even if you narrow your identification down to an oak, you still have to ask yourself, "What kind of oak?" There are over forty different types of oak trees, twenty or more types of maples, and twenty or so types of birches.

Late in the summer, see what kind of fruit the tree bears. If it drops acorns on the ground, the tree is telling you it is some kind of an oak. If the tree drops a nut—sometimes packed into a golf ball-sized casing—the tree may be telling you that it's a walnut or a chestnut or a pecan tree. If the tree's branches are weighted down with apples, peaches, or pears, then that tree is a dead giveaway!

## The Hunt Is On!

Have fun outdoors this summer by trying to see how many trees you can identify without a field guide. Then visit a local library or bookstore where you can borrow or buy a field guide to trees.

As you identify more and more trees in your neighborhood, write their names in a notebook. Trace a leaf from each tree and write a description of the tree's shape, its bark, and any fruit you can see. With experience, you'll get better and better at the tree detective business. And maybe at the end of summer you will have put together your own field guide to trees in your neighborhood.

# Chapter 7
# Autumn in the Air

As the earth rotates on its axis and revolves around the sun, the North Pole periodically tilts toward and then away from the sun. At one point during the year, as the North Pole is halfway between tilting toward the sun and tilting away from it, the planet is straight up and down. That happens on September 23, a day known as the autumnal equinox—the first day of autumn.

On that day, there are twelve hours of daylight and twelve hours of darkness. Because the Northern Hemisphere receives less and less direct sunlight and, therefore, has shorter days, the weather grows cooler during this season.

After the first day of autumn, the North Pole tilts farther away from the sun. Nights get longer and days get shorter. This trend continues until December 21—the first day of winter.

## Autumn Changes Clothes

When the days get shorter and cooler, a lot of trees have to make big changes to stay alive. Other trees don't have to change at all.

Trees are grouped into two categories depending on what they do during the winter. Some trees keep growing leaves right through the cold months. These are known as "conifers," or evergreens, because their leaves stay green throughout the year. Other trees prepare to rest during the winter. They are known as "deciduous," and their leaves change colors in the autumn and fall to the ground before cold weather sets in. (That's the reason autumn is often called "fall" in America.)

## Pigments of Your Imagination

Chlorophyll depends on the sun. So what happens to a leaf in autumn—when the days grow shorter? With less sunlight, the chlorophyll is still broken down and used for food, but it doesn't replenish itself like it did when the sun was beaming down in full force.

And as the chlorophyll production slows because of less sunlight and cooler weather, the supply of chlorophyll in a leaf gradually dwindles. That's when carotenes make their move. The green skin of the leaf begins to fade, and the yellow, orange, and red shades that are produced by the carotene pigments take over.

## A BRIGHT IDEA

Light is what gives a tree the energy to make its own food. Trees absorb light through their leaves, giving them strength to "chew" and "eat" their own food. This process is known as photosynthesis.

So how do trees "chew" when they don't have teeth? Actually, all a tree has to do is catch its food, and photosynthesis helps the tree put that food to good use.

And how does a tree catch its food? With a net. Thousands of nets, in fact.

In every leaf there is a layer of tightly packed cells containing chlorophyll. Chlorophyll is a green pigment that helps cells to

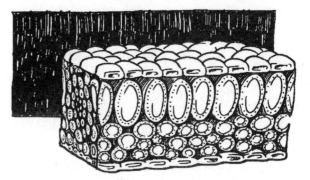

catch the sun's light. The sunlight then breaks down the chlorophyll, along with water and carbon dioxide, to produce the tree's food supply. Chlorophyll makes leaves green.

Even though the chlorophyll is constantly being broken down and "eaten" by the tree, it is also being replaced. As the sun beams down on a leaf, chlorophyll is turned into food energy; meanwhile the leaf uses that energy to make even more chlorophyll.

Leaves of deciduous trees contain a group of coloring pigments in addition to chlorophyll. Called carotenes, these pigments are yellow, brown, and many different shades of orange. As long as chlorophyll is being replenished within a leaf, the carotene colors are hidden by the chlorophyll's bright green.

The leafless tree actually rests through the winter. Like a bear, it hibernates. Resting up and preparing for spring, the branches use the scar tissue, where leaves used to be, to nurse buds that will become next year's leaves.

## Well-Red Trees

Yellow is the most common color of all autumn shades. You probably won't find as many orange or red leaves in autumn—even though they are some of the most beautiful leaves you will ever see. That's partly because the yellow carotenes are stronger than the other carotenes in most trees. But something else has to happen for a tree with lots of orange carotenes to turn its leaves bright red.

Running through each leaf is a tiny vein that carries water from the tree's roots into all parts of the leaf and moves the food produced in the leaf down to the trunk and roots. When chlorophyll is no longer produced in the leaf, a layer of corklike cells forms where the leaf joins the branch. These cells seal off the leaf so that food and water can't flow back and forth. The food sugars that are trapped in the leaf at this point make the leaf turn red.

For the brightest red leaves, a combination of sunny autumn days and cool nights are needed. Sunny days cause the sugar in the leaf to break down, leaving a bright red pigment. Cool nights cause less water from the branch to flow into the leaf. The result is some of the most beautiful leaves of autumn.

## Time to Fall

As the water supply from the branches to the leaves is slowly cut off, leaves turn from green to yellow, orange or red, and then to a crackly, crumbly brown.

When even the leaf stem dries, tissue joining the stem to the branch also dries and gently snaps. Nothing is left to keep the leaf attached to

the tree. Then the lightest of autumn breezes pulls the leaf away from the tree, leaving a scar in the branch, and the dried-up leaf floats lazily to the ground.

### Frosted Flakes

Autumn is usually the season when the first frost occurs. Frost is a layer of ice crystals that forms on everything from plants and grass to windowpanes and outdoor furniture. Sometimes, frost forms in spiky columns. Frost can also look like icy snowflakes.

For frost to occur, three things have to happen:

There must be lots of moisture or water vapor in the air. There must be very little wind. The ground-level temperature must be 32 degrees Fahrenheit (0 degrees Celsius) or less.

Nighttime clouds lessen the possibility of frost. They help cover the sky like a blanket that holds in the heat of the earth's surface. Frost is more likely on clear nights, when there is no "cloud blanket."

God may have made many birds very small, but he also made them very strong. A tiny swallow, which weighs less than half an ounce, flies all the way from Great Britain, where it lives in the summer, to Mozambique, where it lives in the winter. A one-way trip for that bird is five thousand miles! And where does a swallow get so much energy? Most swallows fuel up on a high-protein diet of approximately thirty-six worms, eighteen beetles, and seventy-two seeds!

### Harvest Moon

A harvest moon is the full moon that appears nearest to September 23, the day of the autumnal equinox. It's really like any other full moon, except for three things:

It rises at about the same time the sun sets;
It rises along the horizon instead of straight up into the sky;
It usually has an eery orange glow early in the evening.

Many years ago, farmers started calling it the harvest moon because it remained in the sky longer, giving them extra light at the end of the day to gather in their crops.

The arctic tern migrates farther than any other bird. These birds fly about eleven thousand miles each way between their breeding grounds in New England and Greenland and their winter home in the Antarctic.

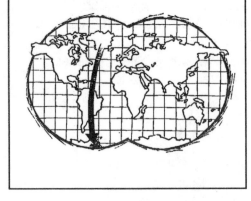

To determine when the harvest moon occurs this year, look at a calendar that shows the monthly phases of the moon. Find out when the full moons occur in September and October. Then, count the number of days between the first day of autumn (September 23) and the first days of the full moon. Whichever full moon is closest to September 23 is the harvest moon.

### Going South: The Autumn Migration

Long ago in ancient Greece, people of all ages used to gather on the banks of the Mediterranean Sea on cool autumn days. They knew if they waited patiently, they would see the giant cranes begin their journey south over the 400-mile wide body of water. From sailors' reports, they realized these great-winged, long-legged birds spent the winter in Egypt across the sea from Greece.

Although the people believed the giant cranes were large enough and strong enough to make the journey, they didn't think smaller birds—like swallows and larks—could fly that far. Instead, they made up stories to explain why the smaller birds disappeared from Greece in the winter.

Some said the birds hopped onto the giant wings of the cranes and

rode piggyback all the way to Egypt! Others said the birds probably drowned somewhere in the sea. Still others said the little birds stripped off their wings and crawled into holes in the ground, where they hibernated

You would probably be amazed by the speed some birds can fly. One duck—a blue-winged teal—flew more than 3,000 miles in twenty-seven days. And a sandpiper once flew more than 2,000 miles in twenty days!

Other birds make long trips much more slowly. The hummingbird, for example, flies all the way from Canada to the southern part of Mexico—more than 3,000 miles. But it usually takes it several months to reach its destination.

for the cold months. "In the spring," people said, "the birds grow new wings."

The truth is, those smaller birds were a lot stronger than the ancient Greeks thought. Not only did some of the small birds fly to Egypt; some went all the way to the southern tip of Africa. This long trip that many different creatures make from one place to another in autumn is known as a "migration."

### They're Molting! They're Molting!

Birds were created to be strong, but they're also intelligent. When trees begin to shed their leaves, birds begin preparing for a long flight south. They molt. That is, they lose their old, worn-out feathers so new ones can grow. In fact, autumn is the best time of year to find cast-off bird feathers.

The first new feathers to appear form a layer that hugs a bird's body and keeps it warm during the upcoming cold months. Over this layer grow the longer feathers that will protect the bird from wind and rain.

Molting isn't the only change that comes before migration. Birds also eat more, so they can store energy for their long flight. Some put on up to forty percent of their original weight before taking off.

## Monarchs on the Move

Birds aren't the only creatures that migrate. Many insects and animals travel in autumn too.

Butterflies, for instance, are very strong fliers. Monarch butterflies can keep flying for almost five days without stopping. Tens of millions of monarch butterflies migrate from Canada to spend the winter in the southern United States and Mexico.

## The Moose Are Loose!

Even deer, elk, wild goats, and moose travel away from their homes when cooler weather comes. They leave their mountains and hilltops behind for the shelter and food of valley forests. In the spring, they return to the hills to graze on lush, new grass.

During the 1880s in North America, columns of buffaloes—sometimes 100 miles long—migrated across the Great Plains from Canada to Mexico. These herds tramped along in single file, actually wearing grooves into the rocks they walked upon.

Today, vast herds of caribou—as many as 100,000 in a herd—march as far as 200 miles south, sometimes crossing wide rivers and high mountains to reach their winter home.

## Time to Go

How do birds and other migrating animals know when it's time to start packing for their long trips? No one really knows. We also don't understand how these animals manage to return in spring to the exact spot they left.

But we do know *why* they migrate.

Somehow, the animals know that their sources of food become scarce in the winter. So, as winter approaches, they prepare for the long trip to sunnier, warmer lands.

Most animals need plenty of daylight hours to hunt for food. The farther south they go, the more daylight hours they'll have. And that means a better chance of surviving for another year—when they'll begin the cycle all over again.

## Summer in Autumn?

You're well into the cool days of autumn. Some farmers have already gathered in their crops. Some people around the world have already held harvest festivals or, in North America, celebrated Thanksgiving. A lot of trees have lost their leaves, and an autumn frost has stopped the flowers from blooming.

Then, surprise! You wake up one morning, walk outside, and it doesn't feel like autumn anymore. In fact, it feels an awful lot like summer. The days are mild and warm and hazy. Is autumn over already? Did you skip winter and spring completely?

Not at all. You're experiencing "Indian summer." It doesn't happen every year. But sometimes, late in autumn and after the first hard frost, there will be a few days of warm temperatures and summerlike weather.

Why "Indian Summer"? When Europeans moved to North America in the seventeenth century, they learned much about planting and harvesting crops from the Native Americans, whom they called "Indians."

But at times, the Native Americans jokingly played tricks on the newcomers. When the settlers experienced summer-warm autumn days for the first time, some suspected that it was another trick of the Native Americans. Therefore, they called those unexpected warm days "Indian summer."

## AIR, LAND. . . AND SEA!

Birds fly and deer walk. But what about sea animals? Not to be left out, water mammals are known to migrate, too. For example, the northern fur seal swims almost 2,000 miles from the Bering Sea (near Siberia) to the Gulf of Alaska during the last month of autumn.

# Chapter 8
# All About Autumn

### The Feast of Saint Francis

One of the best loved saints is Francis of Assisi, who was born in Italy in 1182. Although he was a fun-loving and wild teenager, at the age of 23 Francis drastically changed his way of life. Instead of becoming a soldier or making a lot of money in his father's fabric business, he devoted himself to building churches and helping the poor.

Many people admire Francis because he loved and respected all living creatures. In fact, some churches still remember him—on October 4—by having church members bring their animals to the church's courtyards, where the parish priest asks God's blessings on them.

For a day you'll never forget, think about visiting a nearby church that celebrates the Feast of Saint Francis. And take a four-legged friend with you! Be prepared to see most anything! Some churches have been known to have all kinds of animals show up on Saint Francis's feast day: cows and horses, chickens and parrots, and pigs, in addition to the usual dogs and cats!

### Flight-Pattern Birds

Have you ever seen a flock of wild geese soaring through a late October sky? If you watch them long enough, you'll see a curious thing: one bird begins to take the lead, then others fall into place behind the leader. Gradually, as all the birds settle into position, the flock is transformed into a giant V written on the sky.

Nobody knows for certain why birds fly in such a pattern. Some scientists guess that the leader, an especially strong bird, creates updrafts as it flaps its wings. Other birds move to the side and just behind the leader in order to take advantage of those updrafts. Those birds, in turn, create updrafts for the next birds, who fly to one side of and just behind them . . . and so on, until the V pattern is complete. Because the updrafts make flying easier, the flock can stay in the air for longer periods of time. Plus, this flight pattern allows each bird to see clearly what is in front of it.

Even strong leaders can get tired after a long trip, though. That's why the lead bird often demotes itself—moving back and allowing another, more rested bird to take its place in the front.

## A-maize-ing Facts About Corn

Did you know that. . .

🌽 corn is also known as "maize"?

🌽 corn is a plant that is native only to North and South America?

🌽 corn was first eaten by people living in what is now Mexico more than 10,000 years ago?

🌽 maize was so important to the ancient Aztecs, Incas, Mayas, and other native American people that some of them considered it a gift from the gods? They conducted ceremonies and dances to encourage the gods to make the young corn plants grow.

corn was a word used in Europe during the sixteenth century to refer to different kinds of cereal grains, like wheat, oats, and barley? It is still used this way in some places today.

each kernel of corn is a seed that can grow into a corn plant?

each year, more than 400 million metric tons of corn (over 160 pounds for every person on the planet) are produced worldwide on more than 310 million acres of land—an annual harvest of 15 billion bushels?

there are many different kinds of corn: dent corn, flint corn, flour corn, popcorn, and sweet corn, just to name a few?

"Indian corn" has colored kernels—some black, blue, and red as well as white and yellow?

there are all kinds of uses for corn? It is used to make livestock feed, vegetable oil, meal, flour, grits, soap, and even gasoline (ethanol) for our cars.

corn sugar is used to make syrup?

corn is also used to make cornstarch that, in turn, can be used to make medicine, laundry starch, glue, paper, and textiles?

## Halloween History

The first Halloween celebrations were probably held more than two thousand years ago by a group of people known as Celts. The Celts, who lived in what is now Ireland, England, Scotland, and northern France, held a festival on their new year's eve, which was October 31. To the Celts, the new year marked the beginning of cold and dark days. So it was probably natural that, on the night of this festival, the Celts honored Samhain, whom they believed was the god of death. According to the Celtic priests, Samhain allowed the souls of people who had died the year before to return to their homes on that night.

Because the Celts were afraid of these souls, they blew out all their candles and put out all their fires so that their houses were completely dark. They hoped that the roaming souls could not find their former homes in the pitch-black dark.

Then the people gathered in the center of the village square to build a huge bonfire, which they thought would scare the souls of the dead away from their village.

## The Romans Take Over Samhain

In A.D. 43 the Romans took control of the land where the Celts lived, and they combined two Roman festivals with the Samhain celebration. One of these festivals honored the dead; the other honored the Roman goddess of fruit and trees. (It was during this time that apples became such a big part of October 31 celebrations.) Over time, the Romans turned the Samhain celebration into an autumn feast day on which people ate at huge banquets and then watched or participated in games and races.

## All Hallows' Evening

Later, after many of the people in that part of Europe became Christians, the leaders of the church moved the religious holiday called "All Saints' Day" from May to November 1. The church leaders did this so that people could continue the widely celebrated autumn festival they had observed before becoming Christians. When this happened, the church leaders started calling the evening before All Saint's Day "All Hallows' Evening." The name was soon shortened to "All Hallow E'en," which is how the day became known as "Halloween."

Although church people continued some of the customs of Halloween, they also changed some of the meanings of those customs. For example, the Celts had built bonfires on Halloween because they thought the fire kept scary dead souls away. Hundreds of year later, Christians, too, built bonfires on Halloween. But they said the fire was to keep the devil away, not dead souls.

## "Trick or Treating"

The American tradition of "trick or treating" goes back to the old days of England.  Halloween, which was sometimes called "Nutcrack Night" or "Snap Apple Night," was a time for families to sit around the fire, tell stories, and eat apples and nuts. Then on All Souls' Day—November 2, when the church honored the dead—the poor people would go "a-souling," which meant they'd go door to door begging for food.  They were given pastries called "soulcakes" in exchange for promising to pray for the dead.

So when someone dresses up in a costume and goes door to door saying "Trick or treat," and their neighbors, supposedly to keep them from playing a trick on them, give treats such as candy, fruit, or small toys, they are carrying on an ancient autumn custom.

## The Legend of Irish Jack

For hundreds of years people have been making jack-o-lanterns for Halloween.  This custom is said to have come from an old legend about an Irishman named Jack O'Grady.

As the story goes, Jack (sometimes called "Irish Jack") was a mean and selfish man.  For a long time, the devil had been trying to think of a way to take his soul.  When the devil finally made his move one Halloween night, Jack tricked the devil into letting him live another year.

The next Halloween—exactly one year later—the devil showed up right on schedule.  As Jack walked toward his home on a dark and lonely road, the devil suddenly pounced down in front of him.

"Once and for all," the devil said, "I've come for your soul. I've left the gates of hell open so that I could march you straight in!"

"Now wait just a minute," Jack answered him.  "Surely you've got me this time.  There's no need to rush."

Then Jack looked beyond the devil to where the moonlight was shining on an apple tree. "Before we go," Jack said, "wouldn't you like to taste one of those shiny red apples over there? It's been said those are the sweetest apples in this whole country. Why don't you climb that tree and pick yourself one, and throw me down one while you're at it. After all, I'd sure hate to go to hell hungry!"

The devil didn't see any harm in climbing the tree to pick a couple of apples. Come to think of it, he was feeling a bit hungry. But no sooner had the devil climbed the tree than Jack pulled a knife from his belt and carved a cross on the tree's trunk. Even though Jack was mean and selfish, he was also clever. He knew the devil was more afraid of crosses than anything else in the world. So Jack trapped the devil up in the apple tree.

"You've tricked me," the devil cried.

"Sure have," Jack replied with a laugh. "And I guess you'll just have to stay in that tree forever—or until we can make some kind of deal."

"What kind of deal are you talking about this time?" the devil asked, fuming.

"I'll tell you what," Jack said. "If you'll promise to never take my soul—and I do mean never—I think I can find a way to get you down."

At first, the devil said he'd never make such a deal. But eventually he got tired of sitting up in the apple tree. So he finally gave in and agreed to Jack's deal.

Jack carved the cross out of the trunk of the tree and allowed the devil to come down.

Before the next Halloween, however, Jack died. When he knocked on the pearly gates of heaven, the angels turned him away because he had lived such a mean and selfish life. So Jack turned around and started his journey toward hell. On the way he stopped in the old country and dug himself a turnip to eat. He still had the turnip in his hand when he arrived at the gates of hell.

But the devil refused to let him in.

"Don't you remember my promise, Jack?" the devil asked with a grin. "I couldn't take your wicked old soul even if I wanted to."

"If they won't let me into heaven, and you won't let me into hell, where am I supposed to go?" Jack asked.

"You've nothing else to do but to roam the earth!" the devil shouted. With those words, Jack shrugged his shoulders disappointedly and turned to leave.

"Irish Jack!" the devil called. "Here's a little something to keep you warm." Then the devil threw a red hot coal at Jack. The Irishman caught the coal with one hand, but it burned so badly that he stuck the coal deep into the turnip he was eating.

As the legend goes, Irish Jack still roams the earth, carrying a hot coal in a turnip for a lantern to light his way, still looking for a place to rest. And that's why carved turnips—and nowadays carved pumpkins—are called jack-o'-lanterns on Halloween.

## Your Own Jack-O'-Lantern

Although the original jack-o'-lantern was made from a turnip (and large turnips are still used in some countries), Irish settlers who moved to the United States found that pumpkins were bigger and easier to carve. Ever since, pumpkins have been a regular part of Halloween celebrations.

When you're shopping for a pumpkin to carve, choose a tall or plump one with plenty of room for a big face.

Once you're home, practice sketching pumpkin faces on paper—scary ones, funny ones, maybe even ridiculous ones—before you try the real things. (If you make a mistake on paper, just erase it. If you make a mistake on the pumpkin, you may end up with a weird pumpkin.)

One more thing. Before you begin, cover your work area with several newspapers. Pumpkins may be dry on the outside, but they're wet and slippery on the inside. (A word of caution: Don't carve your pumpkin more than three days before Halloween. After four days, a carved pumpkin will start to decay. And not many people want a shriveled-up pumpkin on display on Halloween night!)

Ask an adult to help you cut the round lid out of the top of the pumpkin. Be sure to cut the lid at an angle—like the left side of the letter A—so the lid will fit onto the pumpkin. Then use a spoon— or, if you're really brave, your hands—to scoop out the pulp and seeds.

Now you're ready to carve the eyes, nose, and mouth.

These holes that you carve into the pumpkin do more than just give your pumpkin a face. Later, when you put a candle inside, they'll allow oxygen to enter the pumpkin and keep your candle burning.

Once you've carved the expression on your pumpkin, you might want to add a few extra touches to make your jack-o'-lantern really shine.

Add hair, eyebrows, or a mustache by gluing on strands of colored yarn.

For extra sparkle, sprinkle glitter over a thin line of glue around the eyes, nose and mouth.

Add jagged teeth by pressing large pieces of raw carrots into the edges of the mouth.

Let your imagination run wild!

Now you're ready to place the candle inside. To keep the candle standing upright, scrape a round crater in the bottom of the pumpkin just wide

## A SNACK FROM JACK

Carving a jack-o'-lantern for Halloween can be lots of fun—even when you have to pull all that slippery, slimy stuff out of the middle. But don't throw that stuff away. There's a great snack hiding in there: pumpkin seeds!

To turn the seeds into a snack, separate them from the pumpkin pulp and wash them off with running water. (Don't let any seeds escape down the drain!)

Next, preheat the oven to 250 degrees Fahrenheit (120 degrees Celsius). Put the washed-off seeds in a bowl, and pour two tablespoons of vegetable oil over them. Stir this mixture around for a few seconds, coating the seeds. Then spread the seeds on a cookie sheet, and bake them for thirty minutes.

Take the seeds out of the oven and allow them to cool. Now you're ready to munch on a high-energy snack that is rich in protein, minerals, and fiber!

enough for your candle. (Be careful not to scrape all the way through the bottom.)

Put a short, wide candle in the pumpkin, and you're all set for Halloween. And if your friends wonder how all this pumpkin carving ever got started, turn off the lights and tell them the story of Irish Jack as your own jack-o'-lantern flickers in the darkness.

### Thanksgiving Day

Thanksgiving is a day set aside each year in America and Canada to thank God for a bountiful harvest. That's why this holiday takes place in autumn after all the crops have been gathered in. It is usually celebrated in special church services and by families who gather together to prepare and feast on a huge dinner.

It's hard to imagine what the people who celebrated the first Thanksgiving had gone through when they finally sat down to their meal. These colonists—called Pilgrims—left England in September 1620 for the long voyage on the ship Mayflower. They reached the New World sixty-five days later, on November 21. Then they explored the shoreline of what is now the state of Massachusetts and decided, exactly one month later, to settle down and build a colony on the land next to Plymouth Harbor.

Winter was hard on the Pilgrims. The cold weather made many of them sick. Those who remained well had to work hard and long to build shelters for the settlement. Food was in short supply. In fact, half of the colonists who made the voyage to Plymouth died before the winter was over.

But in the spring, help came. The Native Americans who lived in that area brought food to the Pilgrims and showed them new ways to hunt and fish. They also showed them new ways of planting and harvesting small crops.

The harvest of 1621 was so big that the Plymouth colonists wanted to celebrate. The Pilgrims planned a three-day festival to thank God for taking care of and providing for them. They also invited their new friends who had helped them grow such a plentiful harvest.

On the days of the feast that took place during the autumn of 1621, long tables were filled with corn bread, duck, eel, goose, leeks, shellfish, venison, watercress, and wine. As the Pilgrims and the Native Americans celebrated their first harvest together, they called that celebration "Thanksgiving."

## Thanksgiving in the United States

Thanksgiving Day became a national holiday in the United States in 1863, when President Abraham Lincoln proclaimed the last Thursday in November as "a day of thanksgiving and praise to our beneficent Father." In 1939, the United States Congress passed legislation that the fourth Thursday of November would be observed as Thanksgiving Day.

## Thanksgiving in Canada

Thanksgiving Day in the provinces of Canada is celebrated earlier than in the United States. That is partly because the harvest occurs earlier in Canada than it does in most of the United States. In 1957, the Canadian parliament proclaimed the second Monday in October as Thanksgiving Day.

## Thinking About Thanks

What are you thankful for this year? Food? Friends? Family? Are there too many things to name?

Or maybe this last year has been a difficult one, and Thanksgiving Day doesn't seem so special after all. Maybe, like the Pilgrims, you've gone through good times and bad times; happiness as well as sadness. Remember that, although they suffered, the Pilgrims never gave up hope. They believed that God was still caring for those who made it through the rough times—teaching them how to live in their new land, providing kind friends, and blessing their hard work.

The Pilgrims had a lot to be thankful for. You probably do too! Why not make it a point this year to tell God, your family, friends, teachers—whoever—that you really appreciate what they've done for you. (It's bound to make *everyone* feel good!)

## Chapter 9
# Autumn Is For. . .

### Making a Leaf Scrapbook

All those beautifully colored leaves of autumn last only a few weeks. Then they dry up and turn brown. But there is a way you can preserve them so that they keep their original autumn color. Make them part of your own personal leaf scrapbook.

The first thing you'll need for a leaf scrapbook are the leaves, of course. So go outdoors and find a place that has many different kinds of trees. If you live near woods or a forest, you've got a great place to find many kinds of leaves. If not, you may have to do a little more walking and searching. Wherever you go, try to pick up as many different colors and shapes as you can find.

Once you've collected the leaves, take them home and flatten them between sections of newspapers. (Be sure to put something heavy on top of them to make sure the leaves are pressed flat.) Then wait eight to ten hours. By then, your leaves should be flat enough for your scrapbook.

Cut sheets of clear adhesive-backed plastic into rectangles that are eight-and-a-half inches wide and eleven inches long (21 cm x 282 cm). Then lay out the plastic so that the sticky side is up, and arrange your leaves on it however you want. (Don't put the leaves too close to the left edge, however. Later on, you will punch holes on that side.) Once you have positioned your leaves, cover them with a second sheet of plastic, sticky side down. This will seal your leaves inside.

Press down hard on the plastic with your palms. Around the edges of the leaves, press especially hard with your fingertips. If you see any air bubbles, squeeze them out through the edges of the plastic.

Finally, select a binder for your leaf scrapbook. Put the sheet of preserved leaves alongside the binder's rings, and measure where you need to make holes along the left side. Then, using a hole-puncher, make holes in the sheet. Place the sheet into the binder, and the first page of your leaf scrapbook is finished!

But don't stop there. Add as many pages as you like. If you know the names of the trees represented in your scrapbook, you can write those names on small pieces of paper or labels and tape them beside the proper leaves. (If you don't know the names of the trees, check your library or bookstore for a field guide to trees. An excellent one is *A Field Guide to Trees and Shrubs* by George A. Petrides.)

## Dried Apple Slices

Autumn is a great time to go walking in the woods. Green leaves are gradually changing into a beautiful array of red, yellow, and orange, dried leaves make loud crunches when you walk on them, and all kinds of nuts can be found around the trunks of some trees.

As you spend some time walking through and maybe even exploring the woods, it would be a good idea to take along a nutritious snack. Rather than buying a snack at the store, you can make your own. Apples, for instance, are plentiful in autumn, and dried apple slices make a delicious treat.

To make dried apple slices, collect six big, juicy apples. Any kind will do, but it would be nice to have a variety of tart and sweet flavors. (Try Granny Smith, Red and Golden Delicious, Cox, Jonathan and McIntosh for starters.)

With a knife, core and then cut the

apples into very thin slices. Do not peel the apples; the peelings are high in fiber and nutrients.

Arrange the slices on a screen or a large baking sheet so they do not overlap. Carefully place the sheet in your oven and set the temperature to 150 degrees Fahrenheit (65 degrees Celsius). Tape a note on the front of the oven so no one will disturb the apples as they dry.

In about eight hours the apples will be done, and you will have a chewy, delicious snack that is rich in vitamins A and C and potassium.

## Nutty Butter

You've got this tremendous craving for peanut butter. You lick your lips as you think about its smooth texture and delicious taste. Before you know it, you're out of your chair and into the kitchen, scavenging through the cabinets and fighting back a snack attack. All you can come up with is a bag of fresh peanuts and a jar of peanut oil. But no peanut butter.

What are you going to do?

Why not make your own? If you've got peanuts, some peanut oil, and a blender, you've got everything you need to make your own peanut butter.

Here's how:

Fill an 8 oz. measuring cup (100 g) with freshly roasted, shelled peanuts (salted or unsalted). Then pour the peanuts into the blender. Using a measuring spoon, add one-and-a-half tablespoons of peanut oil to the peanuts in the blender.

Then, turn on the blender. (Don't forget to place the top on. If you don't, most of your peanut butter may end up on the ceiling!) Blend this mixture until it looks smooth, and then stop. Add another one-and-a-half tablespoons of peanut oil. Blend this mixture for a few more seconds. You're done!

## EUREKA! IT'S PEANUT BUTTER!

A doctor from St. Louis, Missouri, wanted a nutritious snack for his elderly patients. But it wasn't easy to find a snack that they could chew. When one of his patients mentioned how he missed the taste of peanuts, the doctor got an idea. Using the same recipe described above, he made peanut butter.

He loved it! His patients loved it! And millions of people since have loved it too!

Eat your homemade peanut butter your favorite way. But if you're adventurous, try eating it in a way you never have before. Want some ideas? Try a few of these:

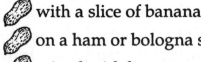 with a slice of banana

on a ham or bologna sandwich

mixed with honey and spread on an apple

on a chunk of sweet pickle

between two vanilla wafers

on your favorite ice cream

on a marshmallow

Store your leftover peanut butter in an airtight jar. And don't be surprised if the oil and peanuts separate after a day or two. It's perfectly natural, and it doesn't mean anything's wrong. Just stir the peanut butter well to mix the oil back in. And enjoy it!

### Squirrels Go Nuts for Acorns

In autumn, squirrels not only eat acorns that fall from oak trees; they also store away many acorns for the winter. But depending on how long the cold days of winter last, many squirrels may fail to store enough food away. By creating an acorn warehouse, you can help the squirrels have all the food they need for the winter.

The best time to look for acorns is during the latter days of October and the early days of November. Most acorns will have fallen from the oak trees by this time, and the squirrels will have had a chance to stock up on their own.

With a large bucket in hand, look under oak trees for fallen acorns. As you find some, pick them up and drop them in your bucket. If acorns are plentiful, you may want to fill more than one bucket. Leave your buckets of acorns outside. Cover the tops of the buckets with aluminum foil.

When winter comes—especially the cold days of January and February—scatter several handfuls of acorns somewhere outside one of your windows. Then, when the squirrels come to eat the food you've provided, you'll be able to watch them. And maybe they'll look up in gratitude, with little eyes that seem to say, "Thank you very much!"

## Making a Quill Pen

When birds molt—when they lose their old, worn-out feathers so new ones can grow—their old feathers are carried off by the wind. Sometimes, you can find them blowing across the ground.

Since autumn is the best time of the year to find cast-off bird feathers, it is also the best time of year to make a quill pen like those used long ago.

To make a quill pen, find a long, discarded feather. Use a knife to whittle one side of the quill until it is flat. Then use the point of the knife to carve a short, narrow slit down the length of the flat side of the quill. Dip the tip of the quill into an ink well, and you've got an ink pen just like ones that were used hundreds of years ago.

## Apple Heads

Apple pie. Apple cobbler. Apple cake. Baked apples, stewed apples, raw apples. Autumn is the season for apples, and you can use them to make all sorts of wonderful things—even little apple people!

Here's how you can turn an apple into a head that's sure to turn heads—and draw the admiration of your family and friends.

Use a sharp paring knife to carefully peel away all the skin on a large apple. Then cut small, shallow indentations where you want the eyes and nose to go, and make a narrow slit for the mouth. (Curve the slit up for a smile, down for a frown.) If you'd like a head with lots of wrinkles, make a number of shallow slits across the "face" area on the apple.

Now it's time to add features to the flesh. To make dark and beady eyes, press cloves, small seeds or black-eyed peas into the eye holes you carved. Use a different kind of seed for the nose. If you'd like to give your head pearly little teeth, press grains of rice into the mouth slit. Make sure that you press the cloves, seeds and rice tightly into the apple flesh.

Then give your head a lemon facial. Pour lemon juice into a bowl just large enough to hold the apple. Soak the head in this bowl for one hour, making sure it is completely covered by the juice.

Remove your apple head and place it in a warm, dry spot to age. In four to six weeks, your apple will have shrunk, dried and withered into a head with character. Check it every day to see the aging process in action. (To speed up the aging process, eliminate the lemon bath and place your apple head in a warm oven—150 degrees Fahrenheit, 65 degrees Celsius—for eight hours.)

Once the head is completely dry, add a few finishing touches to give it real personality. Add hair made of yarn or steel wool. Tack on a lace or fabric collar. Rub a bit of lipstick onto its cheeks. Top it off with a small cap or a doll's hat.

Now your apple head is ready to be admired. Display it on the dining room table for a stunning centerpiece, or (if your parents object) show it off on a shelf in your own room!

## An Autumn Tip for Preserving Creation

One of the ways you can help to preserve creation is to conserve energy. Back in the old days, people used to burn wood for heating and cooking, burn oil for lighting and ride horses for transportation. Well, a lot of things have changed since then!

Now we use gas and electricity for heating and cooking, electricity for lighting, and automobiles for transportation. The discovery of new ways to use these energy sources has been great. But when we use too much energy, our carelessness can cause the earth to become more polluted and can lead to the depletion of our natural resources.

Here are a few tips that you and your family can use to help conserve energy and use energy more wisely:

If your house is already at a fairly comfortable temperature, don't use heaters or air conditioners. Save such appliances for when you really need them. At night, turn off the lights when you leave a room—unless, of course, that means leaving someone in the dark! Don't leave water running when you brush your teeth or wash dishes. Use the water you need, turn it off, and turn it on again if you need more. Walk or ride your bike to nearby destinations, instead of asking for a car ride. The exercise will be healthy for you; and leaving the car in the garage will be more healthy for the environment.

# Chapter 10
# Winter Watch

### Reason for the Season

It's cold—and it's getting colder! Fish begin swimming in the deepest (and warmest) parts of their streams, rivers, and lakes. The growth of most plants either slows down or stops.  Insects are nowhere to be found.  There are still a few seed-eating birds around, but most have flown south.  The food supply for some animals has dwindled so much that many find a place to hibernate until the cold weather is over.

Winter has arrived!

Ever since September 23, the North Pole has been tilting away from the sun. That has made the weather grow cooler in the Northern Hemisphere.  Finally, the North Pole leans as far away from the sun as it ever will in the course of a year.  The day on which this happens—December 21—is known as the winter solstice and marks the first day of winter.  On that day, there are fewer hours of daylight than on any other day of the year. (Which means there are more hours of darkness than on any other day of the year.)

After December 21, the North Pole begins to tilt toward the sun again. The days gradually get longer and the nights shorter. Even so, the temperature continues to drop after December 21. Because there has been less time for the sunlight to heat up the earth's surface, temperatures fall to their lowest points during the winter.

## A Long Winter's Nap

When the weather turns very cold and the food supply dwindles, some animals find the warmest spot they can and settle in for a long nap, spending the winter months in a sleepy, inactive state called hibernation. When animals hibernate, their heart and breathing rates slow down a lot—to a level much lower than during any other time of the year. This long sleep helps them to survive until spring.

Scientists have discovered a special chemical in the blood of warm-blooded hibernating animals that apparently triggers the need to hibernate. If this chemical is injected into a hibernating animal during the summer—when the animal is still active—the chemical will cause the animal to hibernate out of season.

## Which Animals Hibernate?

Hibernating animals come in two classes: warm-blooded hibernators and cold-blooded hibernators. Warm-blooded animals store up body fat to help them survive the cold winter months when they will sleep very much and eat very little. "Warm-blooded" means that they maintain a steady body temperature regardless of the air temperature. Once they settle in for their winter's hibernation, however, their body temperatures fall to a level that helps them sleep. Apparently, a chemical inside their bodies tells them when it is time to hibernate.

A cold-blooded animal's body is just as warm or cold as the air around it. So when the weather gets colder, their bodies get colder— even before they begin to hibernate. When their body temperatures reach a certain low level, these animals begin their hibernation.

### *Warm-blooded Hibernators*

| | | |
|---|---|---|
| Bats | Hedgehogs | Squirrels |
| Bears | Marmots | Swifts |
| Chipmunks | Nighthawks | Woodchucks |
| Hamsters | | |

### *Cold-blooded Hibernators*

| | | |
|---|---|---|
| Frogs | Snakes | Turtles |
| Lizards | Toads | |

Most animals don't really sleep straight through the winter. They have "bouts" of sleep. A bout is a combined period of sleeplike hibernation and wakeful hibernation. Animals do sleep for long periods of time, but they also have shorter periods of time when they are awake but don't move around much.

Some animals store food in the place where they hibernate. That way, during their wakeful time, they can eat a little snack before dozing off again.

## Digging in for the Winter

Most animals like to hibernate in the warmest places they can find. Many animals—both warm- and cold-blooded—prefer to hibernate underground. A ground squirrel curls up into a ball in a hole underground and goes to sleep. A snake usually crawls into the deepest hole it can find; the farther away from the surface it can get, the better. A bear prefers to hibernate in a cave or beneath a tree—sometimes in a hole around the tree's roots.

Frogs and turtles, on the other hand, hibernate at the deepest end of a pond. At times, they even dig into the ground beneath the pond to protect themselves from the cold above. Bats, as you could probably guess, hibernate in caves.

## How Do They Do It?

Because a hibernating animal is so inactive while waiting out the cold months, it needs very little energy to make it through the winter. During autumn, these animals eat a little more than they actually need for a daily diet. Using the extra food, they store up fat in their bodies. Then, while sleeping through the winter, they live off the extra fat.

## Rise and Shine!

Heat is the signal that tells animals it's time to wake up. Sometimes the heat is provided by the spring sun. Some-

times the heat comes from their own bodies. The difference depends on whether the animal is warm-blooded or cold-blooded. A woodchuck, for instance, is a warm-blooded hibernator. After several months of hibernation, its body warms up all by itself—sometimes several weeks before the end of winter. Woodchucks have been known to come out of their winter hibernation homes while there is still snow on the ground.

A snake, on the other hand, stays buried in its hole until warmer weather comes. Cold weather makes a snake's body stiff. If a snake were to come out of hibernation early, it could find itself so frozen it could hardly move.

Snow helps us in at least three ways.

❄ 1. Snow is an important source of water. When snow melts in the spring, the water runs into streams and rivers, increasing the water supply for all living creatures.

❄ 2. Snow adds nutrients to the ground.

❄ 3. Even though snow is very cold, it is also a good insulator. A blanket of snow over plants and hibernating animals can protect wildlife from the cold winter air.

## Let It Snow, Let It Snow, Let It Snow!

What would winter be without snow? There's something almost magical about the way those downy flakes turn the gray drabness of winter into a shimmering wonderland of snowmen, snowballs, and sledding. And what kid doesn't keep her fingers crossed for that special winter bonus: a really heavy snow that clogs the roads and closes schools? Winter without snow would be sad indeed.

But what is snow, anyway? Where does it come from? And how is it formed?

Snow forms from water vapor, but it is different from rain and sleet. For snow to form, the water vapor

inside a cloud has to freeze so quickly that the vapor doesn't have time to become liquid. (If the water vapor becomes a liquid before it freezes, sleet—or frozen rain—is usually the result.)

When water vapor freezes quickly, it forms tiny pieces of ice about the size of dust particles, too small to see without a microscope. At this

point, we don't have snow yet; all we have are tiny ice particles. But then an amazing thing happens.

As tiny ice particles are tossed around by the wind inside a cloud, they crash into and stick to one another. As some of the particles stick to each other, they get heavier and begin to fall. But the wind catches them just as they leave the cloud and tosses them back up, where they crash into and stick to other ice-particle combinations. When tiny ice particles cling to other ice particles, they form snowflakes.

When snowflakes get too heavy for the wind to toss them back up into a cloud, they drift and dive and dart toward the ground. It's snowing!

## Snow Explorer

Wilson Bentley was an American snow explorer. A lot of his neighbors in nineteenth-century Vermont just thought he was nuts. When it began to snow, Bentley would run outside at the same time his neighbors were running indoors.

"The man must be crazy," some neighbors said as they wiped their steamed-up windows and looked out at Bentley. Even during New England blizzards, he could be seen outside trying to catch and photograph snowflakes.

But one day Wilson Bentley accomplished something his neighbors never thought possible. On January 15, 1885, Bentley caught and photographed a snow crystal through a microscope.

Later, after taking more than 6,000 photographs of snowflakes, Bentley came to believe that no two snow crystals were the same. (Scientists have since proved that Bentley was right: no two snowflakes are identical.)

Bentley's photographs made snowflakes very popular. Some people examined Bentley's pictures and then designed jewelry in the shape of snowflakes. Others used his pictures to make snowflake designs on wallpaper and curtains and furniture upholstery.

Soon, the man many people thought was crazy became world famous!

## R(ain) x 6 = S(now)

Have you ever watched the rain on a winter day and wished it were snow? Have you ever wondered just how much wonderful snow that rain would make? There is an easy way to find out.

First, find out how much rain fell. Some newspapers print this information. Or you can measure for yourself. Place a bowl or cup in your lawn to collect the rain. Then use a measuring stick to find out how much you've collected. Once you know how many inches—or fractions of an inch—fell, multiply that amount by six. There's your answer.

For example, if you measure a day's rainfall of two inches, you'll know that if the upper atmosphere had been cold enough, about twelve inches of snow would now be covering your lawn.

## Starry, Starry Night

Star gazing is an ancient activity. Farmers used to watch the stars to know when to plant their crops. (The shifting positions of stars in the sky signaled the changing of seasons.) And night travelers used to watch the stars to tell them what direction they were going. (Probably the best known of those ancient night travelers used a star to guide them to a manger on the very first Christmas.)

You can be a star gazer just for the fun of discovery. Of course, you can see stars any season of the year. But during the winter, when there is less haze (because the earth is absorbing less heat), the atmosphere around the earth is usually clearer. And this gives you the best view of the heavenly bodies. So dress warmly and step outside to gaze at the night stars!

## A Place to Watch

If you live in a city, you will probably have a harder time seeing some of the stars. That's because cities have lots of lights, and those lights may distract your view of the sky. The country is a great place to gaze at the stars. There are few lights, and the stars will seem even brighter.

Regardless of whether you live in the city or the country, stand in the darkness of the night for a few minutes. This will give your eyes some time to adjust to the darkness. Then, when you look up at the sky, the light of the stars will seem brighter and clearer. (If you need to have a flashlight with you, cover the end with clear red film or tissue. This will protect your star-watching eyes from the changes your eyes naturally make when they go back and forth from light to darkness.)

If you stare at the stars for a long period of time, it may seem as if they're moving. Just like our sun, other stars seem to rise in the east and move across the sky until they set in the west. In reality, the stars are stationary; they stay in one place. It is the earth's rotation that makes stars look as if they are slowly moving across the sky.

## Star Bright

When you star watch, you will notice that some stars shine more brightly than others. The brightness of a star is called its "magnitude." But just because one star looks bigger and brighter than another doesn't mean it has a higher magnitude.

Here's why.

The brightness of a star depends on two things: the amount of light energy it releases and its distance from the earth. (By the way, a star's size has little to do with how much light energy it releases.)

A very strong star that is far away may not seem as bright as a weaker star that is much closer to the earth. On the other hand, some faraway stars are so strong that they appear brighter than stars that are much closer to us.

You'll probably also notice that some stars have different colors than other stars. Their colors can tell you something about the temperature of a star's surface.

For example, the surface of red stars—like the star called Betelguese (pronounced "Beetlejuice")—is around 5,000 degrees Fahrenheit (2,760 degrees Celsius). The surface of yellow stars—like our very own sun— is about 10,000 degrees (5,538 Celsius). Blue stars—like the star called Rigel—are the hottest of all. Their surface temperatures are as high as 50,000 degrees (27,760 Celsius)!

## Star Stories

Long ago, people who liked to watch stars began seeing patterns in clusters of stars, much like how we see patterns in clouds today. To those ancient stargazers, some of these patterns looked like people, such as a warrior or a hunter. Other patterns looked like animals—a dragon, bear, or giraffe.

These star patterns came to be called "constellations."

Soon people were telling stories about the starry figures they saw in the sky. As they told their stories, they gave the constellations names,

Some constellations have been given nicknames over the years. For instance, you may be familiar with the Big Dipper and the Little Dipper. Although most people call these constellations by their nicknames, astronomers use their original names, which are Latin for Big Bear and Little Bear: Ursa Major (the Big Dipper) and Ursa Minor (the Little Dipper).

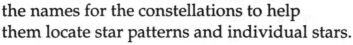

often of heroes from Greek mythology—like Andromeda, Orion, and Perseus. Astronomers—scientists who study the stars—still use the names for the constellations to help them locate star patterns and individual stars.

## What Stars When?

Some stars and constellations can be seen in the night sky year round. Others change with the seasons. And unfortunately, there are some stars in the sky that you can never see (unless you take a trip to the opposite hemisphere).

To help you identify both individual stars and constellations, see if a local bookstore sells star wheels. A star wheel is designed so that you can see which stars and constellations will be visible in your hemisphere during each season of the year. You can also find many good books on astronomy at a bookstore and the library.

## It's *Cold* Outside

You're standing outside in the middle of winter. Even though you are wearing a heavy coat and a warm cap, your face is exposed to blustery winter winds. The thermometer says it is twenty-five degrees Fahrenheit (-4 degrees Celsius), but your cheeks are telling you it's colder than that. Is your face mistaken? Or is the thermometer broken?

Probably neither. Your cold face is experiencing the effects of wind chill.

Meteorologists only recently developed what is now known as the "wind chill factor." The wind chill factor measures the effect that the wind, in addition to cold temperatures, has on your body. In essence, the wind blowing toward your body can make the temperature feel colder than it really is.

Wind chill has become so important because scientists discovered that your body loses heat when the wind blows against it. The more the wind blows, the more body heat you lose.

This is fine in the summer. In fact, you'd probably welcome a breeze then. It helps to keep your body at a more comfortable temperature. But in the winter, you want to keep your body heat in instead of trying to cool down.

## Chapter 11
# Winter Magic

### Christmas

Perhaps you have heard the Christmas song that says, "It's the most wonderful time of the year!"  People hustle and bustle through stores and shopping malls looking for gifts for their friends and family members.  Adults make plans for huge, delicious meals—with Christmas cookies, candies, and punches to follow.  Homes are decorated with pine branches, mistletoe, holly leaves, and lots of lights.  Parties are thrown and church services are attended by millions of people all around the world.

No wonder so many people consider Christmas the most wonderful time of the year!

All this merry-making is because a baby named Jesus was born long ago in the town of Bethlehem, in the Middle East.  Christmas is the celebration of Jesus' birth.  The Bible tells why.

After God created the world and filled it with plants and animals, he created people to care for it.  But the people disobeyed God, damaging their special relationship with him.  So God gave them laws to live by that would help to heal that relationship.  More important, he promised that one day he would send someone who would restore people's relationship with God once and for all.

That someone was God's own Son, Jesus.  Jesus was born in a stable because his earthly parents could find no place else to stay when they traveled to Bethlehem. Not a very impressive way for God's Son to enter the world!

But even in those humble surroundings, Jesus' birth was filled with beauty and marked by wondrous events. A choir of heavenly angels filled the night sky with light and joy as they announced his birth to shepherds on a nearby hillside. Drawn by curiosity and hope, those shepherds left their flocks and went to kneel in wonder before this baby.

Later, wise men from a distant land followed a mysterious new star to the home of the infant Jesus. They, too, knelt in wonder before this promised child, offering him gold, frankincense, and myrrh—costly gifts fit for a king.

Christians celebrate Jesus' birth at Christmas with church services, decorations, music and parties. By giving gifts to one another, they remember the most wonderful Christmas gift of all—God's own Son.

## A Day for Celebrating!

Much of the world celebrates Christmas on December 25. But that doesn't mean Jesus was really born on that date. No one knows the date—or even the month—of Jesus' birth. So why was December 25 picked as the date for Christmas?

The beginning of Christmas celebrations goes back to the time of the Roman Empire. Romans celebrated a holiday called Saturnalia on December 25. This holiday came just after the winter solstice, when the days were short and the nights were long. One of the ways they celebrated the holiday was by lighting candles, lamps, and torches.

In the fourth century, a missionary named Augustine was sent to England to tell the people about the life and teachings of Jesus. Pope Gregory, the leader of the church, told Augustine to continue celebrating the ancient festivals of the people, but to give them new meaning by using them for Christian holidays.

Once in England, Augustine learned that the people celebrated a

Although most countries celebrate Christmas on December 25, the dates for the Christmas holiday were later changed by church leaders in some places. For instance, many countries in eastern Europe celebrate Christmas on January 6. In Armenia, people celebrate Christmas on January 19.

festival on December 25. This festival was based partly on the Roman Saturnalia celebration and partly on a Scandinavian winter celebration. Rather than stopping the people from merry-making, Augustine and other church leaders in England at the time encouraged the people to celebrate the date as the birthday of Jesus Christ. And instead of telling the people to stop practicing festival rituals—such as lighting candles, decorating their homes with greenery, giving presents, and eating special foods—the church leaders made these practices part of Jesus' birthday celebration.

The new holy day caught on quickly. Churches in England began having a special worship service called Cristes maesse, which means "Mass of Christ," to celebrate Jesus' birth. After a few years, the name for this worship service began to be used for the holy day itself. Soon, most of Europe was celebrating "Christmas" on December 25.

## The Story of Saint Nicholas

On Christmas Eve, so the story goes, a jolly old man dressed in red and white travels the world leaving presents beneath Christmas trees for good boys and girls. His method of travel: a sleigh pulled by a pack of flying reindeer. His tool: a sack full of toys slung over his shoulder. His method of entry into children's homes: down the chimney. A description of his face: bright red dimples and a long, white beard. The man and the legend: you probably call him "Santa Claus" or "Father Christmas."

But how did this story start?

Actually, the story of Santa Claus began hundreds of years ago—back in the fourth century. At that time, a man named Nicholas served as a church bishop in the city of Myra, located near the present-day city of Finike, Turkey.

Legend says that, while carrying out his church duties, Nicholas learned of a poor man and his three daughters. This family was so poor that they lived in a broken-down home and sometimes did not have enough food to eat. And even though the oldest daughter was approaching the age at which she could marry, her father had so little money that he could not afford to pay her dowry, the sum given to her future husband.

The story goes on to say that Nicholas found out about the family's poverty and decided to help them. But he wanted his help to be a secret.

So late one night, Nicholas climbed onto the roof of the family's house and dropped a bag of gold down the chimney. The oldest daughter had hung her stockings by the hearth to dry. As the bag of gold fell down the chimney, it bounced into one of the nearby stockings. Imagine her surprise when she found a bag of gold in her stocking! Now that she had enough money, the oldest daughter was soon engaged and married.

When the middle daughter was old enough to be married, Nicholas snuck up to the family's house on a dark night and dropped a bag of gold inside her window. As he was doing the same for the third daughter, the father of the girls caught him in the act. Nicholas pleaded with the man to keep his identity secret, and the grateful father agreed.

The story of St. Nicholas may account for the modern habit of putting gifts in stockings hung by the fireplace.

### Saint Nicholas, Father Christmas, Kris Kringle, and Santa Claus

For hundreds of years, people in Europe practiced the tradition—said to have started with St. Nicholas—of giving surprise gifts to friends and family members at Christmas. Often they claimed that these surprises had been mysteriously brought by St. Nicholas himself! But in the sixteenth century, the church went through a time of change, and some church leaders tried to downplay the role of saints and traditions.

In England, for example, church leaders urged their people to stop giving surprise gifts at Christmas. The leaders felt that too much attention was paid to St. Nicholas and to gifts, and not enough to the story of Jesus' birth. For a while, many people obeyed. But it wasn't long before the gift giving started again. To partially satisfy the church leaders, people no longer said that it was St. Nicholas who brought the gifts. Instead they chose "Father Christmas," a character from children's plays, to be the one who delivered presents.

Years later, in Germany, the people said it was the Christkindl, or Christ child, who sent Christmas gifts. When this tradition came to the United States, the German name Christkindl was misheard as "Kris Kringle."

Meanwhile, the Dutch had never really given up the tradition of Saint Nicholas. But they had shortened his name to "Class," calling him Sinta Class. When Dutch settlers crossed the Atlantic to live in the United States, English-speaking Americans picked up the Dutch name and slightly changed its spelling and pronunciation. The result was "Santa Claus."

In the nineteenth and twentieth centuries, people began mixing up these names and legends. Today, most people consider Saint Nicholas, Father Christmas, Kris Kringle, and Santa Claus to be one and the same person.

## A Badger Forecasts the Weather

No one has ever been able to tell just how long winter weather will last. But that hasn't stopped people from trying for hundreds of years.

Farmers, especially, have always wanted to know when spring weather will begin. They want to plant their seeds as soon as possible so their crops will have a long growing season. On the other hand, they don't want to plant them too early; a sudden burst of cold weather could kill the plants just as they break through the ground.

Years ago, someone in Germany thought he could tell how long winter would last by watching a badger. Late each winter, he stationed himself near the badger's hole and waited for the creature to show itself. If the badger was ready to crawl all the way out of its cozy underground hole and sniff the air, the man figured that spring must not be far away.

It wasn't long before his idea caught on. Soon people all over Germany were watching badgers to predict the beginning of spring weather. The day on which people watched for badgers to come out of their holes was called "Badger Day."

When some Germans moved to the United States and settled in Pennsylvania, they brought Badger Day with them. But as soon as they settled, they realized that they had a problem. There weren't any badgers in Pennsylvania! Rather than giving up Badger Day, they searched for another animal that could help them predict the end of winter. When they saw an American groundhog come out of its hole at about the same time as the German badger did, Groundhog Day was born! Groundhog Day is observed on February 2.

## Valentine's Day

February 14 is a day for sweets and treats. It's a day for love and romance. It's a day for giving away flowers. It's a day for sending "valentines"—cards expressing your affection.

It's hard to say exactly how this special day began. Two stories offer possible clues.

Back in the third century—so one legend goes—a Roman emperor named Claudius II decreed that the strong young men of the Roman Empire could not marry. The emperor believed that single men made better soldiers. Therefore, he strictly enforced this law. But a priest named Valentine considered the emperor's decree to be ridiculous. So Valentine broke the law by secretly marrying young couples who asked him to. Claudius II found out about Valentine's secret weddings and had the priest executed on February 14, 269.

Another legend tells of an early Christian named Valentine who befriended many children when he told them the story of Jesus. But because Valentine worshipped the one true God rather than the gods of the Romans, the emperor had him arrested and thrown into prison. While Valentine was kept captive, the children he'd befriended tossed him notes of love and encouragement through the bars of his cell window.

## A Winter Tip for Preserving Creation

On one of those days when winter weather has you trapped inside, consider writing a letter to an environmental organization, asking for information about how you can help care for the earth. Most of these organizations have special programs for kids just like you who want to make the earth an even better place to live.

Who knows—you may even want to become a member of an environmental group. Although some memberships may cost as much as thirty dollars a year, your money will support research and action on behalf of nature.

What will you get in return for your membership? Many groups produce magazines with great pictures of wildlife and of people working to protect endangered animals and plants. These magazines are also chock-full of information about conservation issues and tips to help you become involved environmentally at home and at school. Some organizations offer discounts or gifts and toys that remind people about the need to care for creation. Lastly, you'll know that you're supporting educational programs and projects to preserve the earth's environment.

## Environmental Organizations

To decide which of these organizations you would like information from, do a little research. Ask your public or school librarian to help you find out more about each of these groups.

Ask yourself: What do they do? How do they help to protect the earth's environment? What are their specialties? What kinds of programs do they have just for kids?

Once you know the answers, you can decide which ones you'd like to know more about.

*The Cousteau Society* 930 W. 21st Street, Norfolk, VA 23517

*Environmental Defense* Fund 257 Park Avenue, New York, NY 10010

*Friends of the Earth* 530 Seventh Street SE, Washington, DC 20003

*Greenpeace* 1435 U Street NW, Washington, DC 20001

*National Audubon Society* 950 Third Avenue, New York, NY 10022

*National Wildlife Federation* 1412 Sixteenth Street NW, Washington, DC 20036

*Nature Conservancy* 1815 N. Lynn Street, Arlington, VA 22209

*Oxfam* 115 Broadway, Boston, MA 02116

*Sierra Club* 730 Polk Street, San Francisco, CA 94109

*World Wildlife Fund* 1250 24th Street NW, Washington, DC 20037

Many people in England used to believe that birds chose their mates on February 14. Arising from this belief was another: that the first unmarried man seen by an unmarried woman on Valentine's Day would become that woman's husband within a year.

## Writing a Letter

Writing a letter to an environmental organization is simple. But here's an example you might want to use as you write your own letter.

---

[Your Name] [Your Address] [Your City, State, and Zip Code]

To [Organization Name]:

My name is _____ _____, and I am _____ years old. I have been learning and trying out some ways to take care of the earth. I am writing to you because I would like more information and ideas about how I can help make the earth a better place to live. Do you have any special programs just for kids? Could you send me information about those programs?

Also, I think I might be interested in becoming a member of [Organization Name]. So could you also send me information about membership? I have enclosed a stamped and addressed envelope. I look forward to hearing from you.

Thank you for all your work toward making the earth a better place for all of us to live.

Sincerely,

[Your Name]

---

When you send your letter to the environmental organization, don't forget to include a stamped envelope with your address written on it. This will save the organization the cost of postage and will allow them to use their money for improving the environment instead.

# Chapter 12
# Winter Is For...

## A Christmas Tree for Birds

How would you like to invite some birds to help you celebrate Christmas? Because Christmas comes four days after the beginning of winter, birds may be looking for "easy food" to help them stretch out their scant winter supply.

First, choose a tree in your yard with lots of branches. Spruce and pine trees work especially well. You'll attract more birds if you pick a tree that is close to other trees and shrubs, one that provides birds with shelter from harsh winds.

Here are some bird-pleasing ways to decorate your outdoor Christmas tree.

Use a needle and thread to string together cranberries, peanuts, or popcorn. Tie a knot at either end of the string so that the decorations don't slide off. Drape the string of bird edibles around the tree, just as if you were putting garland on your own Christmas tree. Use Christmas cookie cutters to cut ornament shapes out of bread. Thread a loop of string through each ornament, and hang it on the tree. Punch a hole through the center of two jar lids. Sandwich a doughnut between the two lids, and thread a heavy string through all three holes (in the top lid, the doughnut, and the bottom lid). Be sure to tie a thick knot beneath the bottom lid to keep the "sandwich" from falling to the ground. Then hang the doughnut treat onto a sturdy branch of a tree. Loop a string tightly around the bottom portion of a pine cone and tie a knot. Spread peanut butter all over the pine cone. Then roll the cone in bird seed. Tie the pine cone onto a branch of the tree, and you will give your feathered friends a double treat! Make a deep groove around the outside surface of fruits and vegetables such as apples and carrots. Tie a piece of sturdy string tightly around the grooves and hang the edible ornaments from your tree. They will add a nice touch of color, and the birds will like them, too! Don't forget to invite a few meat-eating birds as well. You can provide at least some food for them. Attach strips of bacon rind to Christmas tree ornament hooks and add these to your tree. As a final touch, sprinkle lots of bird seed on the ground around the trunk of the tree—a "welcome mat" for your feathered guests.

## Building a Barometer

A barometer is an instrument that measures the air pressure in the atmosphere. Meteorologists use complex and precise barometers to help them predict changes in the weather. You can build a much simpler barometer that will help you predict weather changes. To do so, you'll need the following items:

*scissors*
*a large rubber balloon*
*a Thermos bottle (or other insulated bottle)*
*a small rubber band*
*white glue*
*a plastic straw*
*a sheet of white notebook paper*
*an empty cereal box*
*a pen*
*a ruler*

Use the scissors to cut off the open lip (the end you blow air into) of the balloon. Take the lid off the Thermos bottle, and stretch the balloon over the opening of the bottle. Make sure the balloon is stretched flat across the opening. Then secure the balloon by placing a rubber band around the neck of the bottle.

The reason you must use a Thermos bottle instead of a glass or plastic jar to build a barometer is because Thermos bottles are insulated. It is important that the air inside the bottle stay at a consistent temperature. If the air temperature inside the bottle varies too much, you could get an inaccurate barometric reading.

Put a drop of glue on the center of the balloon. Place the end of the straw into the glue, so that about 1 1/2 inches of the straw are resting on the balloon and the rest of the straw (a little more than 6 inches) is hanging out over the edge. (You will need to hold or prop up the straw until the glue dries.)

Next, glue a sheet of white notebook paper to the front of a cereal box. Set the cereal box beside the Thermos bottle so that the straw extends across the front of the box. Use a pen to mark the level where the straw goes across the box.

Move the box away from the bottle and put a 0 at the spot where you made a mark. Use a ruler to measure and mark a spot 1/2 inch above the 0 level, and write +1 at that mark. (If you use the metric system, make all your marks about 1 cm apart.) Measure and mark another spot 1/2 inch above the +1 level, and write +2 at that mark. Keep measuring and marking up the side of the box until you reach a level marked +10.

You also need to put negative levels on the cereal box. So use the ruler to measure and mark a spot 1/2 inch below the 0 level, and write -1 at that mark. Measure and mark another spot 1/2 inch below the -1 level, and write -2 at that mark. Keep measuring and marking down the side of the box until you reach a level marked -10. Set both the Thermos bottle and the cereal box side by side near a window where they will not be disturbed. Be sure the straw is extended across the 0 level marked on the box. Now you're set to predict the weather!

Reading your barometer is simple. When the straw points to marks above the 0 level, your barometer is telling you that the weather will likely be fair or will be "fairing off" soon. When the straw points to marks below the 0 level, the weather will likely be cloudy or even stormy.

How does it work? Just like more technical barometers, it works because of air pressure in the atmosphere. When the air pressure is high, there are more molecules in the air outside the Thermos bottle than in the air trapped inside. The denser outside air presses down on the balloon, forcing it into the bottle and raising up the outer end of the straw. Higher barometric pressures generally mean clear, fair weather.

When the air pressure is low, there are fewer molecules in the air outside the bottle than the air trapped inside. The denser air inside pushes against the balloon, causing it to bulge upward, lowering the outer end of the straw. Lower barometric pressures usually mean cloudy, rainy weather.

## Tracking Down Birds and Four-Footed Friends

Winter is a good time for unexpected guests—especially the four-footed kind. If you live near open spaces, a park, or woods—or even in the middle of a busy city—you may have had midnight callers without knowing it.

When the food supply gets low in winter, some wild creatures venture nearer to human homes, hoping for an easy meal of leftovers. The remains of your last dinner may have provided a late-night snack for rabbits, skunks, raccoons, or squirrels.

Just because you haven't seen any of these creatures doesn't mean they haven't come calling. Maybe they visited while you weren't looking. More likely, they came at night while you were asleep.

There is a way to find out which animals visit your neighborhood from time to time—even if you don't see them. But you have to have sharp eyesight. And sometimes you have to be willing to get down on your hands and knees and look closely at the ground. One good way to discover which animals are visiting your yard (or wandering through a nearby park or forest) is to identify the tracks they leave.

Animal tracks are easy to see in the snow. But you don't have to have snow to spot them. All you need is bare ground softened by winter rains or melting snow. (Unless an animal is very heavy, its tracks will be hard to spot on grassy ground.)

A close look at animal tracks can tell you what animal made the tracks, how the animal moves, and the direction the animal was going. If the tracks are fresh, you might even find that they lead right up to the animal itself!

## Around-the-House Animals

You might see some of the following tracks in your own yard. These birds and animals have been known to wander close to houses and people.

*Pigeons.* Like crows and starlings, pigeons like to walk in much the same way humans walk. Their feet are usually short and wide, with their toes spread far apart. One footprint slightly ahead of another shows that the pigeon was walking along the ground rather than hopping, as some birds do. As you follow these tracks, you may come to a place where the footprints stop. Look at the ground about six inches to either side of the last set of tracks. See any marks that look a little like brush strokes? Such tracks may have been made by the pigeon's wings, and they mark the place where the pigeon flew up from the ground.

*Sparrows.* Because sparrows, like swallows and chickadees, perch on tree branches and wires, they have long, narrow feet with the toes close together. On the ground, sparrows make tracks that are almost evenly side by side. That means the sparrow hops along the ground.

*Squirrels.* Tracks with tiny, round, four-fingered hands, and long five-toed feet slightly to the front and sides of the hands are probably squirrel tracks. Squirrels' hind feet are longer and heavier than their front feet.

*Rabbits.* Because of the way a rabbit hops, its longer hind feet go down almost directly ahead of its front feet. If the front feet of the rabbit tracks are side by side, the rabbit was calmly and leisurely hopping along. If, however, one front footprint appears ahead of the other, the rabbit may have been scared and was running away from something.

## Keeping Track of Tracks

Now that you've found some interesting animal tracks, why not collect them? Although you can't just pick them up and put them in a scrapbook, you can keep a permanent record of the tracks you've found. Here are some ideas to get you started:

*Take photographs.* Although you may have to take pictures from several different angles to get the best shot, photographs are the easiest way to "collect" animal tracks. (And if the tracks are in snow, they may be the only way to save them!)

*Make drawings.* If you are artistic, carry some pencils and a small sketch pad as you go track hunting.

*Make plaster casts.* This is possible if the tracks are in soft ground or mud that has frozen. Simply purchase some plaster of Paris from a hardware store, mix it up according to the directions, and gently pour it into the tracks. When it hardens, you'll have a plaster impression you can display on a bookcase or hang on your wall.

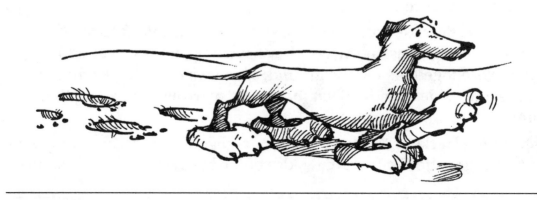

## Recycling Paper

Before hauling off another load of newspapers to the recycling center this winter, why not recycle a few sheets yourself? The experience can teach a lot about how recycling makes paper usable again. And because the whole process can be done in your kitchen, it's a good activity to do indoors when the weather outside is cold.

### *From Paper to Pulp to Paper*

1. Use scissors to shred about fifty sheets of newspaper into very narrow strips. Then cut the strips into small pieces.

2. After sealing the drain, put all the paper pieces into the kitchen sink (or use a large bucket).

3. Cover the paper with water. Let it soak overnight. This will wash the ink out of the paper.

4. The next morning, scoop a little bit of the paper out of the sink and place it in a colander. Hold the colander over the sink to allow the excess water to drain off.

5. This will leave you with wet mush. Collect about seven cupfuls of this mush, and pour them into a large dishpan.

6. Add three cups of water to the mush in the dish pan, and stir this mixture with a large spoon until it is smooth.

7. Add a gallon of water, and continue stirring until the mixture is smooth again. Now you have turned the paper into pulp that can be used to make paper again.

8. Next, slide a rectangular piece of window screen (about eight inches wide and ten inches long) into the dishpan until it is covered by pulp.

9. Holding both ends of the screen, lift it straight up out of the dishpan. Allow the moisture to drain off the screen for about thirty seconds.

10. Place the screen on a table or counter top, and cover the screen with six sheets of dry newspaper.

11. Flip the screen and the newspaper sheets over, so that the sheets are on the bottom and the screen and pulp are on top.

12. Sponge away any water left on the screen. Slowly lift the screen away, leaving the pulp on the sheets of newspaper.

13. Put six more sheets of dry newspaper over the pulp.

14. Use a rolling pin to roll out and press down the pulp between the newspaper.

15. After twenty-four hours, lift up the top layer of newspapers. Peel your recycled sheet of paper off the bottom layer of papers.

16. Finally, try writing on the paper you have recycled yourself.

Does it work? Congratulations! You've just become a paper recycler. Now, let friends and relatives know about your accomplishment by using your homemade paper to make Christmas cards or personal stationery.

## Momentum: The Fast Freezer

Which do you think would freeze faster: hot water, lukewarm water, or cold water? The answer might surprise you.

Try an experiment that will not only give you the right answer, but will also help you to learn something about "momentum." You'll need three bowls, some tape, three strips of paper, and a pen. You'll also need to wait for a day when the outside temperature is below 32 degrees Fahrenheit (0 degrees Celsius).

Using the paper and tape, label one bowl "hot," one "lukewarm," and one "cold." Fill the first bowl with hot water, the second with lukewarm water, and the third bowl with cold water. Carefully carry the bowls outside, and set them down side by side.

Every few minutes, check the bowls to see if ice has begun to form. Maybe even dip your finger into each bowl to test the temperature of the water.

You'll find that hot water turns to ice faster than lukewarm water. Both will freeze before cold water.

It makes sense to think that cold water would freeze first. After all, its temperature is closer to freezing, right? This common-sense thinking doesn't take into account a physical law called "momentum." Momentum affects the actions of tiny moving particles called molecules. The molecules in cold water move around very slowly. Freezing temperatures gradually slow those molecules down until the water freezes solid. The molecules in hot water dash and dart around. When hot water is placed in a below-freezing environment, its molecules slow down very quickly. In fact, they slow down so quickly that the temperature of the hot water falls to the temperature of the cold water and continues to drop! Its temperature will fall so fast that the water freezes even before cold water!

So, the next time you need some ice as quickly as possible, fill the ice trays with hot water. It will turn to ice before cold water would.

# Conclusion

Four seasons make a full year!

As you've experienced and learned more about the four seasons with this book, you've also discovered new ways to enjoy the world and to take care of it all year round. It's good to remember that people are not the only ones who live here. The world was created as a home for trees, animals, birds, insects, fish, and plants as well. What's more, there are generations of people, plants, and animals still to come.

There are at least two things we can do to make certain future discoverers glimpse the wonders and beauty in creation that we've found. First, we can keep enjoying the world and its creatures—learning not to take our planet for granted. Second, we can remember how limited and precious the world's resources are—and do our best to use them wisely.

Christians, people who believe that Jesus Christ was really God's Son and try to follow his teaching, believe that human beings are the best part of creation. According to the Bible, God created people with a special job in mind: to enjoy and care for the world he created.

It's not too surprising, then, that when we do things to make the earth a better place for plants and animals to live, we make the earth a better place for us too.

# Notes

## Notes

## Notes

# Notes

## Notes

## Notes

## Notes

## Notes

## Notes

# Notes

## Notes

## Notes